THE SECRET OF CHARLOTTE BRONTË

FOLLOWED BY
SOME REMINISCENCES OF THE REAL
MONSIEUR AND MADAME HEGER

BY

FREDERIKA MACDONALD, D.LITT.

First published in 1914

British Library Cataloguing-in-Publication Data
A catalogue record for this book is available
from the British Library

CONTENTS

PART I

PART II

Portrait by Richmond

'And now I will rehearse the tale of Love, which I heard from Diotima of Mantineia, a woman wise in this, and many other kinds of knowledge....

'... "What then is Love," I asked: "Is he mortal?" "He is neither mortal nor immortal, but in a mean between the two," she replied. "He is a great Spirit, and, like all spirits, an intermediate between the divine and the mortal." "And what," I said, "is his power?" "He interprets," she replied, "between gods and men; conveying to the gods the prayers and sacrifices of men; and to men the commands and replies of the gods." "And who," I said, "is his father? and who is his mother?" "His father," she replied, "was Plenty (Poros), and his mother Poverty (Penia), and as his parentage is, so are his fortunes. He is always poor, and has no shoes, nor a house to dwell in; on the bare earth exposed he lies under the open heaven, in the streets, or at the doors of houses, taking his rest, and like his mother he is always in distress. Like his father, too, he is bold, enterprising,—a philosopher at all times, terrible as an enchanter, sorcerer, sophist. As he is neither mortal nor immortal, he is alive and flourishing one moment, and dead another moment; and again alive, by reason of his father's nature."'

(*Symposium*. Plato's *Dialogues*. Translator, Jowett, vol. ii. pp. 54, 55.)

THE FRONT OF THE SCHOOL (RUE D'ISABELLE), WHICH REMAINED UNALTERED UNTIL 1909

PART I

CHAPTER I

THE 'PSYCHOLOGICAL PROBLEM' OF CHARLOTTE BRONTË, CREATED BY A FALSE CRITICAL METHOD

We live in an epoch when impressionist methods of criticism, admissible, and often illuminative, in the domains of art and of imaginative literature, have invaded the once jealously guarded paths of historical criticism, to the detriment of correct standards of judgment. Leading critics, whose literary accomplishments, powers of persuasive argument, and unquestionable good faith, lend great influence to their decisions, show no sort of hesitation in undertaking to interpret the characters and careers of famous men and women, independently of any examination of evidence, by purely psychological methods. I am not denying that, as literary exercises, some of these impressionist portraits of men and women of genius, seen through the temperament of writers who are, *sometimes*, endowed with genius themselves, are very interesting. But what has to be remembered (and what is constantly forgotten) is, that if these psychological interpretations of people who once really existed are to be accorded any authority as historical judgments, they must have been preceded by an attentive enquiry, enabling the future interpreter, before he begins to employ psychology, to feel perfectly certain that he has clearly in view the particular Soul he is undertaking to penetrate, with its own special qualities, and placed amongst, and acted upon by, the real circumstances of its earthly career. Where the preliminary precaution of this enquiry, into the true facts that have to be penetrated, and explained, has been neglected, no psychological subtlety, no pathological science, no sympathetic insight, can protect the most accomplished literary impressionist from forming, and fostering, false opinions about the historical personages he is judging from a standpoint of assumptions that do not allow him to exercise the true function of criticism, defined by Matthew Arnold as: 'an impartial endeavour to see the thing as in itself it really is.'

In the case of Charlotte Brontë, her first, and, still, classical biographer, Mrs. Gaskell, carried through, now fifty-seven years ago, with great literary skill, and also with historical exactitude, the study of her parentage and youth; of her experiences in England as a governess; of her family trials and losses; of the sudden development of her talent, or rather, of her genius as a writer, that, at one bound, after the publication of her first novel, made her famous throughout England; and soon famous throughout Europe: and that proved her (since Charlotte has been 'dead'—as people use the phrase—more than half a century, and since her books are still living spirits, we may be allowed to affirm this) one of the immortals.

But now whilst all these epochs in Mrs. Gaskell's *Life of Charlotte Brontë* were studied by exact historical methods, there was one epoch in her heroine's career that this, elsewhere, conscientious biographer neglected to study at all: in the sense, of subjecting facts and events and personages, belonging to its history, to careful examination. Here, on the contrary, we find that Mrs. Gaskell left exact methods of enquiry behind her; and adopted arbitrary psychological methods, of arguments, and assumptions, where, not only no effort was made to consult the testimony of facts, but where this testimony was ignored, or contradicted, when it stood in the way, of preconceived theories. And this period, thus inadequately, or, rather, thus mischievously, dealt with, happened to be precisely the one where the key must be found to the right interpretations of Charlotte's personality; and of the emotions and experiences she had undergone and that called her genius forth to life: and stamped it with the seal and quality that made her, amongst our great English Novelists, the only representative prose-writer in our literature of the European literary movement that French critics praise, and attack, under the name of *le Romantisme.*

The period in Charlotte's life that I am speaking of is, of course, the interval of two years (from Feb. 1842 to Jan. 1844) that she spent at Bruxelles, in the school in the Rue d'Isabelle, whose Director and Directress, Monsieur and Madame Heger, are supposed to have been painted in the characters of 'Paul Emanuel' and of 'Madame Beck,' in the famous novel of *Villette.*

How far that supposition is justified, and to what extent *Villette* is an autobiographical reminiscence, thinly disguised as a novel, can be now, but has never been up to this date, satisfactorily decided, by an attentive historical enquiry. What is established securely to-day, and cannot be removed from the foundation of documentary evidence that serves as the basis upon which all future theorics must rest, is, that it is in this period that Charlotte Brontë—not as an enthusiastic and half-formed school-girl, as some reckless modern impressionist critics, careless of the evidence of facts, would have us believe, but as a woman, profoundly sincere, impassioned, exalted, unstained, and unstainable, who, between twenty-six and twenty-eight years of age, had long left girlish extravagance behind her—underwent experiences and emotions, that were not transient feelings, nor sensational excitements. But they were transforming and formative spiritual influences—causing, no doubt, bitter anguish, and intolerable regrets, that 'broke her heart,' in the sense that they destroyed personal hope or belief in happiness, and even the personal capacity for happiness: yet that from this grave of buried hope, called her genius forth to life; and stamped and sealed it, with its special quality and gift:—the gift that made her a 'Romantic.' So that at this hour one has not to deplore any longer, for Charlotte's sake, this tragical sentiment, of predestined, hopeless, and unrequited love, that broke her heart, but that gave her immortality. For, whilst the broken heart is healed now, or, at any rate, has slept in peace for more than half a century, the genius, born from its sorrow, is still a living spirit; and will probably continue to live on, from age to age, whilst the English tongue endures.

At the present hour all this can be positively affirmed. But even before the final settlement, for every critic who respects historical evidence, of the now incontrovertible fact, Mrs. Gaskell's method of dealing with this momentous period could not satisfy an attentive student who compared her account with Charlotte's correspondence: and also with eloquent impassioned passages in *Villette* and the *Professor*, where the authoress is plainly painting emotions and impressions she has herself undergone. And the effect that was left upon thoughtful readers of the *Life of Charlotte Brontë*' was that the biographer was, not negligently, but *deliberately*, altering the true significance, by underrating the importance, of Charlotte's experiences in Bruxelles, and of her relationships with Monsieur and Madame Heger.

This biographer's theory was (and the doctrine has been vehemently defended by a certain clique of devotees of Charlotte Brontë down to the present day) that Charlotte obtained, certainly, great intellectual stimulus, as well as literary culture, from the lessons of M. Heger, as an accomplished Professor; but that, outside of these influences, her relationships with M. Heger were of an entirely ordinary and tranquil character, and that she carried back with her to Haworth, after her two years' residence in Bruxelles, no other sentiments than those of the grateful regard and esteem a good pupil necessarily retains for a Professor whose lessons she has turned to excellent account.

How far Mrs. Gaskell did believe, or was able to make herself believe, what she professed, it is difficult to determine now. My own opinion is she did *not* believe it; but that she esteemed it a duty to respect the secret *that had not been confided to her*: and to pass by in silence, and with averted eyes, the place where, forsaken by hope, Charlotte had fought out bravely and all alone this battle, with a hopeless passion (that, after all, when it comes across any woman's path, she *must* fight out *alone*, because nowhere, outside of her own soul, is there any help), and then, having won her battle, had gone on, leaving her broken heart buried in that silent, secret place, to face her altered destiny. And to write stories as a method of salvation from despair. But to return, now and again, to visit that silent, secret grave: and to gather the magical flowers that grew there, and breathe their bitter, sweet perfume. And to take large handfuls of these flowers home with her, and, in the air saturated with the bitter-sweet perfume of these magical flowers, to write her stories. So that the stories themselves come to us, not like other stories, but steeped in this strange perfume thrilled through with the magical life belonging to flowers of remembrance, gathered from the grave of a tragical romance. And this explains why the stories are themselves romantic: and why, as Harriet Martineau complained, *Villette*, especially, has this quality, which, to the authoress of *Illustrations in Political Economy*, appeared a defect, that '*all events and personages are regarded through the medium of one passion only—the passion of unrequited love.*'

To return to Mrs. Gaskell and her criticism of Charlotte Brontë. The question of whether she, like Harriet Martineau, committed a critical blunder, as a result of studying Charlotte's character and genius by wrong methods, or whether out of loyalty she endeavoured to cover in her friend's life the secret romance that Charlotte herself never revealed, does not need to trouble us much, because the answer does not greatly matter. However laudatory Mrs. Gaskell's motive may have been, the fact remains, that, as a result of her endeavour rather to turn attention away from, than to examine, the true circumstances of Charlotte's relationships with Monsieur and Madame Heger, an inadequate, or else a false, criticism was inaugurated by her influence of the most popular in Europe of our distinguished women novelists, and who, outside of England, is judged by right standards as a 'Romantic,' but who, in her own country, has been criticised from 1857 down to 1913, in the light of one of two contradictory impressions—both of which we now know were historical mistakes.

The first of these impressions is that Charlotte Brontë has painted, not only her own emotions, but her own actual experiences, in *Villette*; and that Lucy Snowe, Paul Emanuel, and Madame Beck, are pseudonyms, under which we ought to recognise Charlotte herself, and the Director and Directress of the Pensionnat in the Rue d'Isabelle.

The second, and almost equally mischievous impression is that no romantic nor tragical sentiment whatever characterises the relationships between Charlotte Brontë and her Bruxelles Professor in literature; and that she derived her inspirations as a writer solely from the drab dreariness and the desolation of disease and death, of her life in the shadow of Haworth churchyard. It is impossible from the standpoint of either of these impressions to form right opinions about Charlotte Brontë, either as a distinguished personality, or as a writer of genius, whose place in English literature is that amongst our prose writers she is the representative 'Romantic' who counts with George Sand; but differs from her, as an English and not a French exponent of the sentiment of romantic love.

Judged both as a distinguished personality and as a writer of genius from the standpoint of the impression that *Villette* is an autobiographical story, Charlotte Brontë suffers injustice, both as a woman of fine character, and as an imaginative painter of emotions rather than an observer of events, or a critic of manners. Accepted as a realistic picture of her own adventures in Brussels, the book does not testify to her accuracy or skill in portraiture, from the purely literary point of view. And from the moral and personal standpoint, she remains convicted (if she be held to be telling her own story) of the baseness of a half-confession;—and *of a dishonourable and a successful*, not a *romantic and tragical*, love for a married man. And of the treacherous wrong done a sister-woman, who threw open her home to her, when she was a friendless alien in a foreign city. And, if this were so, this traitress would have further aggravated the dishonest betrayal of her protectress, by holding up the woman she had wronged to the world's detestation, either as the contemptible and scheming Mlle. Zoraïde Reuter, of the *Professor*:—or the less contemptible but more hateful Madame Beck, in *Villette*.

If, then, Charlotte did mean, or even suppose, that others could be induced to believe that she meant, to paint her own relationships to Monsieur and Madame Heger in the story, she would stand convicted, not only as a woman of bad character, but as one who had a wicked and vindictive heart.

Nor yet does the second impression, patronised by devotees of Charlotte Brontë (who seem to imagine that the revelation of an entirely innocent and indeed beautiful, though tragical, romantic attachment in the life of this romantic writer, is the disclosure of a sin), help us to find any solution of the 'problem' as psychological critics present it to us, of the 'dissonance' between her personality and dull existence, and her literary distinction, as our chief English Romantic, and the authoress of those amazing masterpieces *Jane Eyre* and *Villette*. What a contrast, in effect, between the characteristics of these masterpieces and the characteristics of her circumstances at Haworth and of the circle of her familiar acquaintances! The characteristics of Charlotte's books are—emotional force, the exaltation of passion over all the commonplace proprieties, the low-toned feelings, the semi-educated pedantries that are the characteristics of the people who surround Charlotte; who are her correspondents and her friends; and whose mediocrity weighs on the poor original woman's spirit (and even on her literary style) like lead:—so that the letters she writes to them are, really, nearly as dull as the letters they write to her; and one finds it hard to believe that some of the letters, to Ellen Nussey, for instance, come from the same pen that wrote *Villette*: or even that wrote from Bruxelles some of her letters to Emily.

And again, if we leave out of account the tragical romantic sentiment for M. Heger, how are we to solve the problem as these psychologists present it to us, and that states itself in this conviction: that the creator of 'Rochester' and 'Paul Emanuel' found her *own*romance, only at forty years of age, in her marriage with the Rev. A.B. Nicholls, an event she announces thus:—'*I trust the demands of both feeling and duty will be in some measure reconciled by the step in contemplation*'; adding on to this the following description of the future bridegroom: '*Mr Nicholls is a kind, considerate fellow: with all his masculine faults, he enters into my wishes about having the thing done quietly*'?

From the standpoint of the impression that the romance in Charlotte's life, was the marriage she speaks of as '*the thing*,' that she wishes '*may be done quietly*,'—and that the highest pitch of personal emotion she attained to, is expressed by her in the temperate confidence that by 'the step in contemplation'—'*the demands of both feeling and duty may in some measure be reconciled*,' (—only *in some measure*? Poor Charlotte!—But she died within a year)—from this standpoint, I say, one really cannot solve the problem of the 'dissonance' between Charlotte's personality and her books.

But there is one conclusion we are bound to reach. The influences of Haworth, no doubt—the drab dreariness of everything; and then the desolation after Bramwell's death, and Emily's death, and Anne's death—and the father threatened with blindness—and also the mediocrity of all those dull, dull people, who represented her familiar friends and correspondents, so satisfied with themselves, all of them; so dissatisfied with life, and who saw it through the medium not of a romantic tragical sentiment, not of one great passion, but through the medium of small grievances of superior nursery governesses: the sort of people who dislike children, and want overdriven mothers to be always occupied with their governesses' sentiments, instead of with the baby who is cutting its teeth. No doubt the influences of Haworth and of Charlotte Brontë's 'Circle' there, before she became famous, *did* help to plant in her the immense depression and fatigue of a spirit that had known the stress of great emotions, and *could bear no more*,—expressed in the letter announcing her decision to marry one of the curates she had laughed at in *Shirley*—who *with all his masculine faults*,' she says, 'is a *kind, considerate fellow*,' who doesn't expect her to pretend she thinks this marriage ('*the thing*')—a Festival. Well, but the conclusion we must form is this, that if it be at Haworth, and after 1846, that we must find the causes of the depression that brought about Charlotte's marriage with Mr. Nicholl, it is *not* here that we must seek the '*Secret of Charlotte Brontë*';—the romance that broke her heart, true—but made her an immortal, whose claim to live for ever is based upon no moderate well-balanced sentiment, where 'the demands of both feeling and duty will be in some measure reconciled'—but upon passionate emotions, compelling expression, and forming a new language almost; as M. Jules Lemaître has said 'introducing new ways of feeling, and as it were a new vibration into literature.'

And in the place where the romance in Charlotte's life is found must we seek, also, the source of this power of emotion: creating powers of expression to which much more accomplished literary artists than Charlotte (Jane Austen and Mrs. Gaskell, for instance) never reached; and to an intimate knowledge of moods and ecstasies and raptures, that rule and torture and exalt human souls, that much more subtle and scientific psychologists than herself (George Eliot, for instance, and Mrs. Humphry Ward) never discovered.

The supreme gift of the authoress of *Villette* and *Jane Eyre*, as a painter of emotions, an interpreter of intimate moods, a witness in the cause of ideal sentiments, an incessant rebel against vulgarity and common worldliness, and the stupid tyranny of custom, an upholder of the sovereignty of romance, cannot be weighed against, nor judged by, the same standards as the accomplished literary gift of such finished artists as the authors of *Pride and Prejudice* and *Cranford*, such subtle students of character as the authors of *Middlemarch*and *Robert Elsmere*, such vigorous fighters for intellectual and moral ends as are represented by the author of the *Illustrations upon Political Economy*, and the *Atkinson Letters*. And it is because, as a result of judging her genius and her personality from the standpoint of false impressions, Charlotte Brontë has not been recognised in England as a painter of personal emotions, a Romantic in short, but has been judged as the advocate of a general doctrine—(one very agreeable to the convictions of the average man, but especially exasperating to the aspirations and principles of the superior woman)—I mean, the doctrine that *to obtain the love of a man whom she feels to be, and rejoices to recognise as, her 'Master,'—is the supreme desire and dream of every truly feminine heart*; it is because, I say, of this mistake, that Charlotte has become the idol of a class of critics least qualified perhaps to appreciate the merits of a romantic rebel against conventional domesticity; whilst amongst more naturally sympathetic judges, the peculiar perfume and power of these novels, steeped in and saturated with the passionate essence of a personal romance, has not been recognised either for what it really is,—the 'magic' of Charlotte Brontë; the special quality in her work that gives it originality and distinction; but this very quality—'the personal note' that makes her our only English Romantic Novelist, has been signalised by many sincere admirers of her books as a defect!

I have already mentioned the judgment passed upon *Villette* by an admirable woman of letters, Charlotte Brontë's personal friend, and a critic whose good faith, and honest desire to serve the interests of this sister-authoress with whom she found fault it is quite impossible to doubt.

When *Villette* appeared, Charlotte Brontë had been for some little time on very friendly terms with Harriet Martineau: and she did not fear to incur the risk—always a perilous one to friendship—of asking Harriet to tell her, quite frankly, what she thought of her book. Harriet responded with perfect frankness to the invitation; and the almost inevitable result followed. The event wrecked their friendship. And no one was to blame: Harriet Martineau, without disguise, but without malice, said what she thought was true. But neither was Charlotte in the wrong, for she felt herself unjustly judged; and her feeling was right, because Harriet used false standards.

'As for the matter which you so desire to know,' wrote the frank Harriet; 'I have but one thing to say: but it is not a small one. I do not like the love—either the kind or the degree of it—and its prevalence in the book, and effect on the action of it, help to explain the passages in the reviews which you consulted me about, and seem to afford some foundation for the criticism they afford.'

Charlotte was deeply offended: 'I protest against this passage,' she wrote; 'I know what *love* is as I understand it, and if man or woman should be ashamed of feeling such love, then there is nothing right, noble, faithful, truthful, unselfish in this earth, as I comprehend rectitude, nobleness, fidelity, truth and disinterestedness.'

Here spoke the Romantic. But Harriet Martineau was *not* a Romantic but an Intellectual, and she judged Charlotte's books and her genius through her own temperament, and by intellectual standards. She followed up the private rebuke to her friend for making too much of love, in a review of *Villette*, contributed to the *Daily News*.

'All the female characters,' she wrote, 'in all their thoughts and lives, are full of one thing, or are regarded in the light of that one thought, love! It begins with the child of six years old, of the opening (a charming picture), and closes with it at the last page. And so dominant is this idea, so incessant is the writer's tendency to describe *the need of being loved*, that the heroine, who tells her own story, leaves the reader at last under the uncomfortable impression of her having either entertained a double love, or allowed one to supersede another, without notification of the transition. It is not thus in real life. There are substantial, heartfelt interests for women of all ages, and, under ordinary circumstances, quite apart from love; there is an absence of introspection, an unconsciousness, a repose, in women's lives, unless under peculiarly unfortunate circumstances, of which we find no admission in this book; and to the absence of it may be attributed some of the criticism which the book will meet with from readers who are no prudes, but whose reason and taste will regret the assumption that events and characters are to be regarded through the medium of one passion only.'

The critical blunder in this judgment is that here the authoress of the *Illustrations in Political Economy* and of the *Atkinson Letters*sees the authoress of *Villette* through her own temperament, as an intellectual like herself:—a humane sociologist, and a philosophical freethinker, *whose literary purpose is to use her talent as a writer in the service of her ideas and principles.* Judging *Villette* and its authoress from this point of view and by these standards, Harriet Martineau decides that *because* 'all events and characters in *Villette are* regarded through the medium of one passion, love,' *therefore* the literary motive and purpose of the authoress must have been to deny—or at any rate to ignore—that '*there are substantial heartfelt interests for women of all ages, and in ordinary circumstances, quite apart from love.*'

The mistake lay in assuming that Charlotte Brontë was an intellectual, instead of an imaginative genius; and that her literary purpose was to affirm, or deny, or ignore deliberately, any principle; or in any way to make her genius the servant of her intellect; whereas her intelligence was so coloured by her imagination, so subservient to her genius, that if one were to measure her by intellectual standards—with Harriet Martineau, for instance—she would remain as vastly Harriet's inferior in enthusiasm of humanity, in practical benevolence and warm interest in social reform, and in emancipations from prejudice and insularity and bigotry, as she was Harriet's superior in power of passionate feeling, in wealth of imagination, and in superb gift of expression. But any such comparison would be out of place. Let us admit that Charlotte's thoughts and aspirations, as we find them scattered through her writings, express the ordinary vigorous prejudices of an English gentlewoman of her period, brought up under the influences of a father who was a good sort of Tory clergyman; that her attitude of condescension toward, rather than of sympathy with, the 'common people,' regarded as the 'lower orders,' who should be kindly treated of course, but kept in their place, and taught to 'order themselves lowly and reverently to their betters,' indicates a defective humanitarianism; that her almost rabid patriotism—her conviction that not to be English is a misfortune, and a stamp of inferiority that weighs heavily as an impediment to nobility and virtue, upon every member of every other foreign race, is distinctly narrow; and that her staunch and straitened protestantism, leaves her as far away as the 'idolatrous priests' she denounced, from any claim to enlightened tolerance.

Yet this lack of any particular height or breadth or distinction in Charlotte Brontë's social, political, critical, or even religious views, does not in any way detract from the height, depth and distinction of her powers of noble emotion and splendid expression; nor from the rare gift of translating words into feelings that quicken her readers' sensibility to a finer perception of the ideal beauty that lies at the heart of common things.

Here is the gift by which we have to judge, or, to speak more becomingly, for which we have to praise and thank, our only English 'Romantic' novelist, who stands in rank with George Sand, and who has been studied in comparison with her by Swinburne. And we have to praise, and thank our Charlotte all the more, because she has a national as well as a personal note: and brings to this European literary movement the characteristic qualities of imagination and sentiment that belong to our English literary temperament, and that do us honour, as a romantic people who are romantic in our own, and nobody else's way.

But now if we want to appreciate the 'magic' of Charlotte Brontë as a Romantic we must not look for the sources of her inspiration at Haworth; nor in the circle of dull people, to whom she wrote, brilliant writer as she was, dull letters, because their mediocrity weighed upon her spirit like lead.

Twenty years ago, now, I attempted (but was not especially successful in the task) to establish upon the personal knowledge that my own residence as a pupil in the historical Pensionnat in the Rue d'Isabelle, at Bruxelles gave me of the facts of Charlotte Brontë's relationships to Monsieur and Madame Heger, right impressions about the experiences and emotions she underwent between 1842 and 1846, and that supply the key and clue to the right interpretation of her genius. Every opinion I then ventured to state, not upon the authority of any special power of divination or of psychological insight of my own, but solely upon the authority of this personal knowledge of Monsieur and Madame Heger in my early girlhood, and also of the information I owed to the friendship and kind assistance given me, in my endeavour to rectify false judgments, by the Heger family, has quite recently, not only been confirmed, but established upon entirely incontrovertible evidence, by the generous gift made to English readers throughout the world of the key needed to unlock once and for ever the tragical but romantic 'Secret' of Charlotte Brontë.

CHAPTER II

THE KEY TO THE PROBLEM

The common saying, that 'people must be just before they are generous,' becomes at once less common and more correct when it is formulated differently. '*One needs to be very generous before one can be really just*' is Jean-Jacques Rousseau's way of stating the proposition. And one calls this sentence to remembrance when recognising how much generosity is revealed in the act of justice recently performed by Dr. Paul Heger in his gift to the British Museum (that is to say to English readers throughout the world) of the four tragical, but incomparably beautiful, Letters written by Charlotte Brontë to his father, the late Professor Constantin Heger, within two years of her return to England.

No doubt this gift *was* an act of justice. Without the conclusive evidence these Letters afford, there would have been no means of rectifying the arbitrary, false, and inadequate criticism of the personality, and thus, indirectly, of the writings, of a great novelist misjudged especially in her own country.

But whilst, for these reasons, the publication of these Letters was a duty to English literature, the son of the late Director and Directress of the Bruxelles Pensionnat—unwarrantably supposed to have their literal counterparts in the interesting Professor Paul Emanuel, and in the abominable Madame Beck—might well, in view of the unintelligent and ungenerous criticism of his parents by English readers, have refused to recognise any obligation on his side to concern himself with the rectification of the dull laudatory, or the malicious condemnatory, judgments passed, from a false standpoint, on the authoress of *Villette.*

We find Dr. Paul Heger able to rise entirely above all personal rancour, and to recognise that Charlotte Brontë herself is not to be made responsible because a good many of her critics have blundered. Indeed, the conduct of the whole Heger family since the publication of *Villette*, and the death of Charlotte Brontë, has been distinguished by this fine spirit of disinterestedness; and by a dignified indifference to undeserved reproaches. The answer to all charges, of unkindness to Charlotte on Madame Heger's part, or of injudicious kindness first, followed by heartless indifference, on M. Heger's side, was in their hands; and they had only to publish the present Letters to establish the facts as they really were. But this could not have been done in the time when *Villette* appeared, nor even immediately after Charlotte's death, without wounding others. *Villette* appeared in 1853. In 1854 Charlotte, then in her fortieth year, married the Rev. A.B. Nicholls; and she died less than a year after this marriage. Mr. Nicholls survived her more than forty years. No doubt he would have been wounded in his sensibilities by the disclosure of his late wife's entirely honourable, but very romantic and passionate earlier attachment to somebody else. Intimate personal friends of Charlotte, also, would have been afflicted, not by her revelations, but by the commentaries upon them that a certain type of critic would have infallibly indulged in. Whilst these conditions lasted, the Heger family scrupulously refrained from publishing these documents. Twenty years ago, when I was collecting the materials for my article published in the *Woman at Home*, and when, in the light of my own recollection of M. and Madame Heger, as their former pupil, I endeavoured to rectify, what *I knew to be*, false impressions about their relationships with Charlotte Brontë, I was told by my honoured and dearly loved friend, Mademoiselle Louise Heger, about the existence of these Letters; *but they were not shown me.* And I was further assured that, whilst they would be carefully preserved, they would not be published, until every one had disappeared who could in any way be offended by their disclosure. After the lapse of more than half a century since

Charlotte's death, these conditions have now been reached. And in his admirable Letter to the Principal Librarian of the British Museum, Dr. Paul Heger explains his reasons for making this present to the English people of documents entirely honourable to the character of one of our great writers, and that explain the emotions and experiences that formed her genius:

'Sir,—In the name of my sisters and myself' (thus runs the opening sentence of the Letter reprinted in the *Times*), 'as the representatives of the late M. Constantin Heger, I beg leave to offer to the British Museum, as the official custodian on behalf of the British People, the Letters of Charlotte Brontë, which the great Novelist addressed to our Father. These four important Letters, which have been religiously preserved, may be accepted as revealing the soul of the gifted author whose genius is the pride of England. We have hesitated long as to whether these documents, so private, so intimate, should be scanned by the public eye. We have been deterred from offering them sooner, by the thought that, perhaps, the publicity involved in the gift might be considered incompatible with the sensitive nature of the artist herself. But we offer them the more readily, as they lay open the true significance of what has hitherto been spoken of as the "Secret of Charlotte Brontë," and show how groundless is the suspicion which has resulted from the natural speculations of critics and biographers; to the disadvantage of both parties to the one-sided correspondence. We then, admirers of her genius and personality, venture to propose that we may have the honour of placing these Letters in your hands; making only the condition that they may be preserved for the use of the nation.'

'Doubtless,' continues Dr. Paul Heger, when dealing with the actual relations between Charlotte and the Director and Directress of the school in the Rue d'Isabelle, 'Doubtless, my parents played an important part in the life of Charlotte Brontë: but she did not enter into their lives as one would imagine from what passes current to-day. That is evident enough from the very circumstances of life, so different for her, and for them. There is nothing in these Letters that is not entirely honourable to their author, as to him to whom they are addressed. It is better to lay bare the very innocent mystery, than to let it be supposed that there is anything to hide. I hope that the publication of these Letters will bring to an end a legend which has never had any real existence in fact. I hope so: *but legends are more tenacious of life than sober reality.*'

The last observation shows that Dr. Paul Heger, an experienced *littérateur*, foresaw what has actually happened, and that the defenders of the two 'legends' of Charlotte Brontë, patronised by writers who derive the authority for their opinions about her, not from the study of the facts of her life and character, but from their own impressions and convictions, are not going to admit that the legends are overthrown, simply because it has been proved that they are founded upon mistakes. At the same time, no statement can be more true than that 'facts are stubborn things,' and that, when these 'stubborn things' are found arrayed in stern and uncompromising opposition to the impressions and convictions of the most accomplished psychological theorists—well, it is the psychological theorists who must give way.

And this is the situation that has to be faced to-day by critics of Charlotte Brontë, who have either formed their opinions about her in the light of their impression that *Villette* represents an autobiographical study, or else who have founded their judgments of her personality and genius as a writer upon their conviction that it is a '*silly and offensive imputation*' to suppose that her sentiment for M. Heger was a warmer feeling than the esteem and gratitude a clever pupil owes an accomplished professor.

In connection with the tenacity of life of this last theory (after the publication of the evidence which proves it is a mistake), we have to consider with serious attention the account rendered in the *Times* of the 30th July 1913, of an interview with Mr. Clement Shorter, known to be the most distinguished supporter, in the past, of the doctrine that Charlotte's sentiment for Professor

Heger was 'literary enthusiasm,' and nothing more. And this serious attention is needed, because, in Mr. Clement Shorter's case, it is not allowable to dismiss lightly the judgment of a critic who (after Mrs. Gaskell) has done more than any one else to throw light upon the family history of the Brontës, and also upon and around those three interesting and touching personalities—Emily, Anne, and, the greatest of them all, Charlotte, amongst the familiar scenes and personages of their environment at Haworth, both before and after they had conquered their unique place in English literature. One cannot for a moment suppose that Mr. Clement Shorter wilfully refuses to see things as they really are, simply because it pleases him to see them differently? No! One realises perfectly that, as with Mrs. Gaskell fifty-seven years ago, *so* with this modern conscientious and generous critic to-day there exists an entirely noble, and, *from a given point of view*, justifiable reason, for refusing to handle or examine a matter with which (so it is alleged) historical and literary criticism has no concern—a purely personal, and intimate secret sorrow, in the life of an admirable woman of genius; the sanctuary of whose inner feelings it is by no means necessary to explore: and still less necessary to throw open to the vulgar curiosity and malevolent insinuations of a generation of critics, infected with hero-phobia, and the unwholesome delight of discovering '*a good deal to reprobate and even more to laugh at*,' in the sensibility of men and women of genius, who have honoured the human race, and enriched the world, *because* they have possessed through power of feeling, power also of doing fine work, that the critics who find much in them 'to reprobate and more to laugh at' have not the power even to appreciate. Now, *if* the point of view of Mrs. Gaskell and Mr. Clement Shorter were a correct one, with all my heart and soul I, for my part, should approve of their action in slamming the door in the face of invading facts that threatened to leave the way open for scandal-hunters and hero-phobists to enter with them, and to deal with the honoured reputation of Charlotte Brontë in the same way that—more to the discredit of English letters than to that of two French writers of genius—recent critics have dealt with the love-letters of Madame de Staël and George Sand.

This point of view, however, is a mistaken one in the present case, because, to commence with, Charlotte Brontë's romantic love for M. Heger affords no game to the scandal-hunter; but, on the contrary, it is serviceable to the just appreciation of her character, as well as of her genius, that her true sentiment for her Professor—*that explains her attitude of mind when writing 'Villette'*—should be rightly understood. Then also, whilst Madame de Staël's infatuation for Benjamin Constant neither adds to nor diminishes her claims, as the authoress of *Corinne* and *de l'Allemagne*, to the rank of a fine writer and a great critic, and while George Sand's tormenting and tormented love for the ill-fated, irresistible, unstable 'child of his century,' de Musset, is a poignant revelation of the passing weakness (through immense tenderness) of a splendidly strong and independent spirit, that one is almost ashamed to be made the spectator of, Charlotte Brontë's valorous martyrdom, undergone secretly and silently, and 'rewarded openly,' fills one with an extraordinary sentiment of respect for her: and justifies Mr. Clement Shorter's own fine and generous utterances upon the impression that the Letters that betray the anguish she endured, and overcame, alone, produces upon him.

'*Charlotte Brontë*,' said Mr. Clement Shorter, by the report of an interviewer who recorded his opinions in the *Times*, 30th July, immediately after the publication of these Letters, '*is one of the noblest figures in life as well as in literature; and these Letters place her on a higher pedestal than ever.*'

Let me quote from the same report in the *Times* the further statement of his opinions given by this well-known critic, as to the sentiments revealed in these Letters:

> 'Mr. Shorter,' affirmed the interviewer, 'welcomed the publication of the letters in the *Times* "as giving the last

> and final word on an old and needless controversy." "Personally," he said, "I have always held the view that those letters were actuated only by the immense enthusiasm of a woman desiring comradeship and sympathy with a man of the character of Professor Heger. There was no sort of great sorrow on her part because Professor Heger was a married man, and it is plain in her letters that she merely desired comradeship with a great man. When Charlotte Brontë made her name famous with her best-known novel, she experienced much the same adulation from admirers of both sexes as she had already poured upon her teacher. She found that literary comradeship she desired in half a dozen male correspondents to whom she addressed letters in every way as interesting as those written by her to Professor Heger. There is nothing in those letters of hers, published now for the first time, that any enthusiastic woman might not write to a man double her age, who was a married man with a family, and who had been her teacher. When one considers that half a dozen writers have, in the past, declared that Charlotte Brontë was in love with Professor Heger, it is a surprising thing that Dr. Heger did not years ago publish the letters. They are a complete vindication both of her and of his father, and, as such, I welcome them, as I am sure must all lovers of the Brontës."'

In his first contention Mr. Clement Shorter is undeniably right: it *is* quite true that '*the publication of these Letters places Charlotte Brontë on a higher pedestal than ever.*' But why is this true? *Because these are love-letters of a very rare and wonderful character*; because the passionate tragical emotion that throbs through them is a love that, recognised as hopeless, as unrequited, makes only one claim; that, *precisely because it makes no other*, it has a right to be accepted and to live. Now this sort of love is a *very rare and wonderful emotion, that only a noble being can feel; and that although it is hopeless, tragical, is nevertheless a splendid fact, that renders it absurd to deny that sublime unselfishness is a capacity of human nature.* And, again, these letters place Charlotte Brontë 'on a higher pedestal than ever,' because in them her vocation and gift of expressing her own emotions in a way that makes them 'vibrate' in us like living feelings is here carried to its height. So that these personal letters, more even than the pictured emotions of Lucy Snowe, stand out as a record of romantic love that (in so far as I know) has never before been rivalled. It is true we have the romantic love-letters of Abelard and Héloïse, and the letters in the *New Héloïse* of Saint-Preux to Julie, and of Julie to Saint-Preux, after their separation, as beautiful examples of love surviving hope of happiness; and Sainte-Beuve has quoted, as examples of the tragical disinterested passion of a love that claims no return, but only the right to exist, the letters of some eighteenth-century women: Mademoiselle de l'Espinasse, Madame de la Popelinière, and Mademoiselle d'Aissé. But in none of these historic love-letters (so, at least, it seems to me) does one feel, with the same truth and strength as in these recently published letters of Charlotte Brontë to M. Heger, the 'vibration' of this tragical, hopeless, romantic love, that asks for nothing but acceptance, that does not 'seek its own'—the love that only asks to give, compared with which all other sorts of love, that *do* seek their own and claim return, are as sounding brass and a tinkling cymbal.

But now, if we were to accept the view of these letters, that they do not express love at all, but merely the writer's '*desire of comradeship with a great man*': and that '*after she had become famous "she found that literary comradeship she desired, in half a dozen male correspondents, to whom she addressed letters in every way as interesting as those written by her to M. Heger*"'; and that '*there is nothing in these letters that any enthusiastic woman might not write to a man double her age, who was a married man with a family, and who had been her teacher*'—if we could accept all these views, could we *then* hold the opinion that 'the publication of these letters places Charlotte on a higher pedestal than ever'?

It seems to me, on the contrary, that *then* we should find ourselves compelled to admit that Charlotte Brontë had fallen very much in our esteem as a result of the publication of these Letters. For whilst romantic love is a noble sentiment that does honour to the heart that feels it, an '*immense enthusiasm for literary comradeship with great men*' is not *necessarily*, nor generally even, a commendable sentiment. It is very often merely a rather vulgar and selfish persistency in claiming the time and attention of busy people who don't want the comradeship; and I suppose there are very few people in the least degree famous who have not been rightly harassed by the 'enthusiasm' of professing admirers who have nothing to do themselves, and who want busy men or women of letters to correspond with them. And if a desire of comradeship with M. Heger had really been the sentiment and motive of Charlotte's letters to him, after she left Bruxelles, then the fact that she continued to write to him although he did not answer her letters would prove that she was insisting upon being the 'comrade' of some one who did not want her. Again, if the tone and terms of these Letters to M. Heger in 1845 were the same that she employed with '*half a dozen other male correspondents*,' after she became a famous writer, well Charlotte *would* fall in our estimation, both as a writer, who ought to know how to avoid extravagant language, and as a self-respecting woman who should not have allowed her enthusiasm for literary comradeship to induce her to repeat experiences that, without loss of dignity, one cannot pass through more than once in a lifetime.

Happily, however, attention to facts proves that none of the conditions that, if they had existed, would have rendered the writing of these Letters discreditable to Charlotte's reputation, can be accepted as in the least credible. It is not credible that her sentiment for M. Heger was that of intellectual enthusiasm for a great man double her age; because, to begin with, M, Heger was *not* double Charlotte Brontë's age, but only seven years her senior. About this question there can be no dispute. M. Heger was born in 1809; and Charlotte Brontë in 1816. In 1844 Charlotte then was twenty-eight, and M. Heger thirty-five years of age, and given the fact that women lose their youth first, M. Heger had precisely the age that would render him most sympathetic to a woman who was still young but who had left girlhood behind her. Again, M. Heger was not a '*Great Man*,' in the sense of being either a celebrity, or an original genius with gifts or qualities of an order calculated to kindle intellectual hero-worship; and he was further a dictatorial and ingrained Professor, the very last person on earth to offer literary comradeship to a former pupil. The Director of the Pensionnat in the Rue d'Isabelle, and the former *Préfet des Études* at the Brussels *Athénée* (who had resigned this post when religious instruction, made a free subject, was excluded, as a compulsory Catholic training from the college curriculum) was a man of talent, who had weight in Catholic circles, and was recognised in his character of a Professor as one with an admirable gift for teaching, even by the enemies of his religious convictions; but he was not in any way, save as a teacher, a distinguished or famous personage; and in all probability if this English writer of genius had not immortalised him in the character of 'Paul Emanuel,' M. Heger would not have outlived the affectionate and respectful remembrance of his family and personal friends.

The method of testing the question of whether intellectual enthusiasm, or tragical romantic love is the sentiment revealed in these Letters is *to read the Letters themselves—in the light of a true impression of the real relationships (when they were written) between Charlotte Brontë and M. Heger*, that is to say in the first twelve months that followed Charlotte's farewell to the Director and the Directress of the Pensionnat in the Rue d'Isabelle, in January 1844. And to obtain this right impression, we have to see what had taken place, to alter the original entirely friendly terms between Madame Heger and the English under-mistress, who during the first year of her stay in Brussels had been a parlour-boarder:—for the story told in *Villette* of Lucy Snowe's arrival at the Pensionnat in the Rue d'Isabelle late at night, and with no place of shelter, having lost her box and been robbed of her purse on the voyage, is, to start with, an incident that has no place in the true history.

CHAPTER III

CHARLOTTE'S LAST YEAR AT BRUSSELS

1842-43

What were Charlotte Brontë's real relationships with Monsieur and Madame Heger when, in January 1844, she bade them, what was to prove, a final farewell? This is what has to be understood before we can read with a full sense of their true meaning the tragical impassioned Letters to M. Heger, written within the first two years of Charlotte's return to England, Letters that not only place the authoress of *Jane Eyre* and *Villette* (as a devotee, and an exponent of Romantic love) on a 'higher pedestal than ever,' but that, also, explain at what cost of personal anguish she attained as a writer her extraordinary power of translating emotions into words, that, by the impression they produce retranslate themselves to her readers' imagination and sensibilities as feelings.

We have always to remember that the relationships between Charlotte and her former Professor were not those that existed between Lucy Snowe and her 'Master.' Paul Emanuel was unmarried, and in love with Lucy, although Madame Beck and the Jesuit, Père Silas,—and in the end Destiny—prevented the love-story from reaching a happy ending.

Nor were these relationships, as the facts of the case reveal them, those imagined by Mr. Clement Shorter; where '*it was no cause of grief to Charlotte that M. Heger was married*,' because her enthusiasm for him was that of simple hero-worship for a great man. Nor yet were these relationships, when she left

Bruxelles in 1844 (nor had they been for some ten months before that date), the same relationships (of trustful friendship on the one hand and sympathetic interest on the other) that had existed between Charlotte and the Director and Directress of the Pensionnat in the Rue d'Isabelle when, a year earlier (in January 1843), Charlotte had returned to Bruxelles alone, *in response to Madame's as well as Monsieur's invitation*, to perfect her own French, and to receive a small salary as English Mistress. These first relationships had continued untroubled for the first few months after Charlotte's return. Thus, in March 1843, writing to her friend Ellen Nussey, she qualifies her complaints of loneliness in the Pensionnat (without the companionship she had enjoyed the previous year of her dearly loved sister Emily) by reference to the kindness of Madame, as well as of Monsieur Heger.

'As I told you before,' she writes, 'M. and Madame Heger are the only two persons in the house for whom I really experience regard and esteem; and of course I cannot be always with them, nor even very often. They told me, when I first returned, that I was to consider their sitting-room my sitting-room, and to go there whenever I was not engaged in the schoolroom. This, however, I cannot do. In the daytime it is a public room, where music-masters and mistresses are constantly passing in and out; and in the evening I will not, and ought not, to intrude on M. and Madame Heger and their children. Thus I am a good deal by myself; but that does not signify. I now regularly give English lessons to M. Heger and his brother-in-law. They get on with wonderful rapidity, especially the first.[1]

So that, up to this date, no cloud is visible. But by May 29 there is a cloud above the horizon. It is no bigger than 'a man's hand' as yet: but it is charged with electricity, and one knows the storm is gathering. This time Charlotte is writing to Emily, *who never liked M. Heger for her part*. 'Things wag on much as usual here, only Mlle. Blanche and Mlle. Haussé are at present on a system of war without quarter. They hate each other like two cats. Mlle. Blanche frightens Mlle. Haussé by her white passions, for they quarrel venomously; Mlle. Haussé complains that when Mlle. Blanche is in a fury "*elle n'a pas de lèvres.*" I find also that Mlle. Sophie dislikes Mlle. Blanche extremely. She says she is heartless, insincere and vindictive, which epithets, I assure you, are richly deserved. *Also I find she is the regular spy of Madame Heger, to whom she reports everything. Also she invents, which I should not have thought.* I am [not] richly off for companionship in these parts. *Of late days, M. and Madame Heger rarely speak to me; and I really don't pretend to care a fig for anybody else in the establishment.* You are not to suppose by that expression that I am under the influence of *warm* affection for Madame Heger. *I am convinced she does not like me: why, I can't tell.* (O Charlotte!) *Nor do I think she herself has any definite reason for this aversion.*(!) But for one thing, she cannot understand why I do not make intimate friends of Mesdames Blanche, Sophie and Haussé. M. Heger is wondrously influenced by Madame: and I should not wonder if he disapproves very much of my unamiable want of sociability. He has already given me a brief lecture on universal *bienveillance*; and perceiving that I don't improve in consequence, I fancy he has taken to considering me as a person to be let alone, left to the error of her ways, and consequently he has, in a great measure, withdrawn the light of his countenance; and I get on from day to day, in a Robinson Crusoe like condition, very lonely. That does not signify; in other respects I have nothing substantial to complain of, nor is even this a cause of complaint. *Except for the loss of M. Heger's goodwill (if I have lost it,) I care for none of 'em.*'[2]

Let us see what this letter, written eight months before Charlotte left Bruxelles, tells us about the altered facts of the relationships between herself and the Directress and Director of the School. First, it is no longer Monsieur and Madame Heger who are the only people Charlotte cares about in the establishment, *but it is only the goodwill of M. Heger that she would grieve to lose.* And Madame Heger, who so kindly invited her to consider the family sitting-room hers, now takes no notice of her, and, Charlotte knows it, has taken an aversion to her. And when M. Heger says, 'Don't you think, "Mees Charlotte," who is lonely without her sister Emily, should be taken more notice of?' Madame Heger replies coldly: '*If "Mees" is lonely, it is her own fault. Why does she not make friends with her compeers, Mesdemoiselles Blanche, Sophie and Haussé?* They are of her rank; they follow the same profession; no, this young Englishwoman is full of the pride and narrowness of her race! She is without *bienveillance*: she esteems herself better than others, she makes her own unhappiness; *and it is not for her good to single her out amongst the other excellent under-mistresses as we have done.* Let her make herself friends amongst them: *let her learn to be amiable.*' And M. Heger, who thinks there is something true in this, because his unalterable opinion is that it belongs to the English character, and to the Protestant creed, to be proud, narrow, unamiable and without benevolence, lectures Charlotte in this sense. Here are the facts of the situation in May 1843.

Now what has happened in these few months to so change the relationships between Charlotte and Madame Heger, and to render Monsieur Heger—*under Madame's influence*—less friendly and helpful than he had formerly been, in his efforts to encourage the studies, and brighten by gifts of books, and talks about them, the solitude of the English teacher? It is not very difficult to discover the cause of the change, if only critics with psychological insight would employ this quality, not to fabricate problems out of false impressions, but to penetrate the true significance of the evidence that lies open to one, of the actual circumstances and facts.

The circumstance that explains the fact of Madame Heger's altered conduct and feeling towards the English under-mistress whom only a few months earlier she had invited to use her own sitting-room, and to regard herself as a member of the family, and whom *now*she scarcely speaks to, and thinks should find companions with the other under-mistresses, is a discovery that Madame probably made, before even Charlotte herself had fully recognised what had happened. This discovery is that a change has taken place in Charlotte's sentiment towards her 'Master in literature'; a sentiment that at first had not transgressed the limits of a cordial and affectionate appreciation of his kindness and of his talent and charm and power as a teacher—approved of by Madame Heger as a becoming sentiment in this young person, convenient, 'convenable.' But as Charlotte's exclusive pleasure in M. Heger's society and conversation increases, with her distaste for the society and conversation of every one else with whom she is now in daily contact, and as the charm of his original personality grows, with her sense of the natural disparity between herself and the self-controlled Directress, whose rule of life is respect for what is *convenient,* in the French sense of *la convenance* (*i.e.* what is *becoming*) and of revolt against the vulgarity and profligacy she finds as the distinguishing characteristics of her fellow-governesses, this sentiment becomes transformed (insensibly and fatally, without her knowledge or will) into a passionate personal devotion—in other words, into a sentiment that does transgress very seriously indeed the limits of the sort of feeling that Madame Heger, in her double character of directress of a highly esteemed Pensionnat de Demoiselles, and of the wife of Monsieur Heger—esteems 'convenient,' in the case of an under-mistress in her establishment. It was not a question of ordinary jealousy at all. Madame Heger, a much more attractive woman than Charlotte Brontë in so far as her personal appearance was concerned, was absolutely convinced of the affection and fidelity of her husband, and of the entirely and exclusively professorial interest he took in assisting this clever and zealous and meritorious daughter of an evangelical Pastor, to qualify herself for a schoolmistress in her own country. It was entirely a question of the '*inconvenience*'—the unbecoming character of this unfortunate infatuation, that renders it entirely intolerable; something that must be got rid of at once; but as quietly as possible, without exciting remark, and with as much consideration for this imprudent, unhappy 'Mees Charlotte' as possible. The whole affair is a misfortune, of course, 'un malheur': but what one has to do, now it *has* arrived, is to guard against even greater 'malheurs' for everybody concerned. For 'Mees Charlotte' herself, first of all—what a 'malheur' should this 'infatuation,' involuntary and blameless in intention, no doubt, but so utterly inconvenient, betray itself in some regrettable exhibition of feeling, most humiliating to herself, and most distressing to her only parent, the respectable widowed evangelical Pastor in Yorkshire! And then for the Pensionnat, what a 'malheur' should any gossip arise: and what sort of an effect would it produce upon the mind of parents of pupils, who most naturally would object to the knowledge of the existence even of a sentiment so inconvenient as this being brought to the knowledge of their young daughters? And confronted with these perils, Madame Heger's conclusion upon the only way of avoiding them, is really not a very unreasonable nor unkind one. It is that the sooner 'Mees Brontë' returns to her home in Yorkshire, the better for herself, and for the interests and the tranquillity of the Director and the Directress of the Pensionnat in the Rue d'Isabelle: who wish to sever their relationships with her on friendly terms; who, in the future, when she has cured herself of this unhappy extravagance (as no doubt her good sense and excellent upbringing will assist her to do) hope to renew their intercourse with her; but who, in the circumstances that have arisen, think it better all intimacy should be suspended.

Nor, having formed this conclusion, was Madame Heger's method of endeavouring to force Charlotte to adopt it also, either wilfully unkind or inconsiderate. Her method was to convey forcibly to Charlotte's knowledge *without any needless humiliating explanations*, that she, the Directress of the Pensionnat where Charlotte was under-mistress, has penetrated the secret of her feelings towards M. Heger, and consequently that the old terms between herself and Charlotte have become impossible, and that the necessity has arisen to assert her claims and to establish the rules that must be observed in the ordering of the Pensionnat and of the staff of teachers for which she is responsible. Without discussions or recriminations in connection with the reasons for this decision, these mere reasons, well known to Miss Brontë herself, convince her that it is not convenient 'Mees' should continue a teacher, or even an inmate, in her school any more; and surely this circumstance alone should point out to 'Mees' herself, what she ought to do? Let her do this, let her take the opportunity offered her of relieving Madame Heger of the painful necessity of touching upon distressing subjects, and the secret they share shall never be made known to any one, *not even to M. Heger himself*, who is entirely unconscious of it. An explanation could easily be found by 'Mees' for the necessity of her return to England:—her aged father's infirmities, the establishment of the school that she is now qualified to manage, etc.—and all this matter will arrange itself quietly. *To bring Charlotte to dismiss herself* was Madame Heger's purpose: but in view of the slowness and reluctance of this obstinate Englishwoman to recognise what was 'becoming,' and expected from her, the immediate object became to guard against any self-betrayal by Charlotte of her state of feeling to other members of the establishment, *and especially to M. Heger,* whom Madame knew to be entirely innocent of any warm feeling resembling romantic sentiment for the homely but intelligent and zealous Englishwoman, whose progress under his instruction and capacity for appreciating good literature made her interesting to him as a pupil, whilst her meritorious courage in working to qualify herself to earn her own bread as an instructress herself claimed his approval—but whom he had not as yet suspected of a tragical passion for him. *And Madame Heger esteemed it most undesirable he should ever make the discovery.* And *therefore* her immediate care was to guard against the occasion of such a revelation being given: and *therefore* she endeavours to stop private lessons given by M. Heger to Charlotte, or English lessons given by her in return; *therefore* too, she works to prevent any intercourse or meetings between the Professor and this particular pupil, outside of the presence of spectators and listeners, whose unsympathetic but attentive eyes and ears will impose restraint upon this extravagant Charlotte; so little under the control of good sense and respect for what is becoming.

But now these tactics followed by Madame Heger, although from her own point of view they were as considerate and judicious as the interests of Charlotte, the Pensionnat, and 'convenience' permitted, and although no personal jealousy, vindictiveness nor malice entered into them, nevertheless *from Charlotte's point of view* were intolerable and cruel; and the torments they inflicted upon her during the long seven months she lived through this incessant conflict with Madame Heger, under cover of an outer show of politeness on both sides, were precisely the same torments of cheated expectancy, suspense, thwarted hope, disappointments, that she has painted in *Villette*, and the *Professor*, as inflicted upon the hapless governesses Lucy Snowe and Frances Henri, by those two cruel, pitiless head-mistresses Madame Beck and Mlle. Zoraïde Reuter. Yes:—but there was all the difference in the world between the circumstances arranged by the authoress in her two novels, and the circumstances as a mischievous destiny had entangled them in the true history.

In the stories made to please her fancy by Charlotte, we have in *Villette* Paul Emanuel unmarried—and in love with Lucy Snowe; but by the base contrivances of Madame Beck, a Jesuit priest, Père Silas, has been called in, to stir up superstitious dread of allying himself with a heretic in the mind of the good Catholic that Paul was, and so prevent him from carrying through certain tentative indications of the state of his affections that have awakened and justified the passionate but timid and self-despising Lucy Snowe. Nothing then can be more plain than the position here—Paul Emanuel and Lucy Snowe are being divided, and trouble is being created, by a horrid, jealous, mischievous Madame Beck, who wants Paul Emanuel to marry her, although she knows he loves Lucy, and that Lucy is in love with him, but too little self-confident, too feeble, in her dependent position, to assert her claims. In the*Professor* it is much the same case, only

Mlle. Zoraïde Reuter is more of a cat than Madame Beck, and less an evil genius, who demands admiration for her cleverness whilst Mlle. Zoraïde, who makes coarse love to the Professor, provokes contempt.

Well but now here is the real case. Madame Heger knows that here is the English daughter of an Evangelical Pastor, who (although she is old enough to look after herself), is nevertheless under her (Madame's) protection, and behold this young woman has taken it into her head to conceive a most inconvenient infatuation for her husband, M. Heger! Now how is one to meet this situation in the best way for everybody? Happily the secret lies between herself and Mees Charlotte: it rests with Mees to take herself out of harm's way: and all is safe. But that is what she will not do. So here you have the position: this grown-up, obstinate Englishwoman, with her 'inconvenient' passion, always on the verge of exhibiting her sentiments in a way that may inform M. Heger—who is the best of men; most honourable, but still a man—who may or may not see how serious this is: who may tell one, 'Let *me* talk reason to her,' which is the last course to take! It is true, Madame will have said to herself, 'I might take matters into my hands; and since she has no sense of 'convenience' herself, I might say: 'Mees, I exact this of you: *immediately* you make up your trunks, and return to Yorkshire; you start to-morrow.' Yes, but what happens then? There are observations,—indignation is excited. M. Heger will say to me, 'What now is this sudden attitude you take up towards Mees? it is not just.' And if I explain, he may say: 'You imagine things; you women are not good to each other.' Or he may say: 'Let *me talk to Mees Charlotte*,' and then there will be *attaques de nerfs*—who can say? No, there is only one thing to do: as this Englishwoman has not herself any sense of 'convenience.' We must be patient until the end of the year, when her term is finished. *Then she goes*, arrive what may. And, meanwhile, one must support it; only she must not meet M. Heger alone: and one must constantly take precautions, in this sense, against scenes.'

Well, was there anything very cruel, or hard-hearted, or vindictive, in Madame Heger's conduct? If you are a psychologist, put yourself in her place. What could she have done with this entanglement of circumstances, all menacing what she most valued, a watchful preservation of 'convenience,' most necessary in a Pensionnat de *Jeunes Filles* of high repute? If any one will suggest a plan that would have been more considerate to Charlotte than the one she took, I should very much like to hear what plan? Even then, in the light of what I know of Madame Heger's incapability of a deliberate desire to torture, or inflict severe punishment on any pupil, or teacher, or living thing, I should still protest confidently that in all she did—that sweet and kind old schoolmistress of mine—in the days when she was twenty years younger than when I knew her—she *meant* to be considerate and kind.

Without attempting to decide who, between Charlotte and Madame Heger, was to blame, or whether either of them were to blame, here, at any rate, we have the conditions of feeling between these two women: each exasperated against the other, under the strain of a forced politeness, during the last seven months of Charlotte's residence in Bruxelles. No doubt, for both of them the strain was great. All this time (without saying it out aloud) Madame Heger was forcing upon Charlotte's attention, the '*inconvenience*' of her presence in the Pensionnat; the necessity for her return to England. All this time Charlotte—outwardly compliant with all the demands made upon her, that keep her writing letters at Madame's dictation (*in the hours when Monsieur is giving his lessons in class*), that send her upon messages to the other end of Bruxelles (*upon holidays when Monsieur's habit is to trim the vine above the Berceau in the garden*)—all this time, Charlotte's bitter protest spoke out in the gaze she fastened on the Directress: 'Merciless woman that you are! *you* who have everything; who are his wife, the mother of his children, whom he loves; who will enjoy his conversation and his society, and the pleasant home you share with him, all your life; and who grudge me—I, who have nothing of all this, but who love him more—I, who in a few months must go out into the dark world, without the light his presence is to me; without the music his voice makes for me; without the delight his conversation is to my mind, and the complete satisfaction his society brings to my whole nature—and you grudge me these few months of happiness? Rich and cruel woman, who, in your selfish life possess all this, you are more cruel than Dives was to Lazarus; you grudge me even the crumbs that fall from your table.'

[1]*Life of C.B.*, p. 254.

[2]*Life*, p. 258.

CHAPTER IV

THE CONFESSIONS AT ST. GUDULE

We are now in a position to realise the emotions and experiences that lasted up to the eve of Charlotte's return to England. But there are two events that vary the incessant conflict with Madame Heger; and that help to form the basis of real experiences, expressed in the portraits (that are not historical pictures) of Zoraïde Reuter and of Madame Beck. These two events also re-appear, as scenes in *Villette, that did not take place in the way the authoress relates* them; but that put us in possession of the parallel facts in Charlotte's true career: where she felt the very same emotions she describes in the novel. The first event gives us the actual, the original history, of what in *Villette* reappears in the imaginary account of Lucy Snowe's Confession: and serves there to introduce us to the Jesuit who is half a spy and half a saint—Père Silas. In Charlotte's life the event, as it is related by her in a letter to Emily, took place during that long and solitary vacation in the empty Pensionnat, where, from August to October 1843, Charlotte was left to face the position now made for her by Madame Heger's discovery of the Secret that, possessed by her enemy, could not remain hidden from Charlotte herself.

Charlotte's letter to Emily begins by describing the desolation of this large house, with its deserted class-rooms, and silent garden, and galérie, and for her solitary companion only the repulsive-minded and malicious Mademoiselle Blanche, whom she has described in an earlier letter as a spy of Madame Heger's.

'I should inevitably,' she writes, 'fall into the gulf of low spirits if I stayed always by myself.... Yesterday I went on a pilgrimage to the cemetery, and far beyond it, on to a hill where there was nothing but fields as far as the horizon. When I came back it was evening, but I had such a repugnance to return to the house which contained nothing that I cared for, that I kept treading the narrow streets in the neighbourhood of the Rue d'Isabelle, and avoiding it. I found myself opposite to *Ste. Gudule*; and the bell, whose voice you know, began to toll for evening *salût*. I went in quite alone (which procedure you will say is not much like me), wandered about the aisles (where a few old women were saying their prayers), till vespers. I stayed till they were over. Still I could not leave the church nor force myself to go home—to school, I mean. *An odd whim* came into my head. In a solitary part of the cathedral six or seven people still remained, kneeling by the Confessionals. In two Confessionals I saw a Priest. I felt as if I did not care what I did, provided it was not absolutely wrong, and that it served to vary my life and yield a moment's interest. I took a fancy to change myself into a Catholic, and go and make *a real Confession* to see what it was like. Knowing me as you do, you will think this odd, *but when people are by themselves they have singular fancies.* A penitent was occupied in confessing. They do not go into the sort of pew or cloister the priest occupies, but kneel down on the steps and confess through a grating. Both the confessor and the penitent whisper very low: you can hardly hear their voices. After I had watched two or three penitents go, and return, I approached at last, and knelt down in a niche which was just vacated. I had to kneel there ten minutes waiting, for on the other side was another penitent, invisible to me. At last that one went away, and a little wooden door inside the grating opened and I saw the Priest leaning his ear toward me. I was obliged to begin, and yet I did not know a word of the formula with which they always commence their confessions!... I began by saying I was a foreigner and had been brought up as a Protestant. The Priest asked if I was a Protestant then. I somehow could not tell a lie, and said yes. He replied that in that case I could not "*jouir du bonheur de la confesse*," but *I was determined to confess*, and at last he said he would allow me, because it might be the first step towards returning towards the true Church. *I actually did confess—a real Confession.* When I had done he told me his address, and said that every morning I was to go to the Rue du Parc to his house, and he would reason with me and try to convince me of the error and enormity of being a Protestant. I promised faithfully. Of course, however, the adventure stops here: and *I hope I shall never see the Priest again.* I think you had better not tell Papa this. He will not understand that it was *only a freak*, and will perhaps think I am going to turn Catholic.'

Only 'a freak'?—an 'odd whim'? Even without the knowledge of the special facts we now possess, could any serious student of Charlotte Brontë believe it? Given what we know of her seriousness, of her religious temper, that cannot take spiritual things lightly, of her rational Protestant piety, of her antipathy to Catholic formulas—given all this as characteristic of her aspirations,—and as characteristics of her personality, shyness, and reserve carried almost to morbidness—can any one believe that mere *ennui*, a craving for variety, excitement, flung this normally shamefaced, timid Englishwoman down on her knees, on the stone steps of the Sainte Gudule Confessional; inspired her with the determination needed to withstand the Priest's objections to allow her, as a Protestant, *de jouir du bonheur de la confesse*; compelled her to insist upon her claim, by virtue of her dire need of this '*happiness*' (or at any rate of this *relief*) of unburthening her soul by a 'real Confession'? A *real* Confession—of *what*? What crime has this poor innocent Charlotte on her conscience that stands in such need of confession? No crime, we may be sure. Only the weight, the misery of this tragic 'Secret'; too intimate, too sacred to be confided even to those nearest to her,—even to Emily. But now that her 'enemy' holds it, too grievous a secret to remain unshared with Some One, who is not an enemy, nor yet a friend—a stranger, who will not blush nor tremble for her, will not see her whilst she whispers through the grating: whom she will not see, or meet again;—Some One, who by profession, is God's Delegate of Mercy to deliver the unwilling offender, who repents him of his secret sins, Some One who is pledged, when he has given pardon and consolation, *never to betray what he has heard—to forget it even.* Some One who, experienced in offering counsel and consolation, may (who can say?) offer some comfort or advice, assisting her to extricate herself from the snare into which she has fallen, and to recover safety.

Does one not know what the 'Confession,' whispered through the grating, really was? Or can one doubt what the Priest's advice was? Was it not necessarily the same advice so urgently forced upon her by Madame Heger? She must escape from the peril of temptation: she must not show this tragic passion any mercy: she must break this spell: she must go back to England. She felt she could not do this thing of herself without 'God's special grace preventing her'? Therefore she must diligently seek to obtain this grace *by the aid of the Holy Catholic Church*—and she must call in the Rue du Parc—next morning. In so far as the last recommendation went, we know Charlotte did not follow it. *The adventure*—as she says herself, *stopped there.* Nor is there anything in her own story to indicate the existence of any real Jesuit, taking the place of the mischief-making Saint, Père Silas, familiar to readers of *Villette.* The Priest of Ste. Gudule comes to us as a more impressive personage just because Charlotte *never met him again.*

But his advice remained vividly present to her recollection we may feel sure. On the 23rd October, about a month after this event, she writes once more to Ellen Nussey:—

'It is a curious position to be so utterly solitary in the midst of numbers. One day lately I felt as if I could bear it no longer *and I went to Madame Heger and gave her notice. If it had depended upon her I should certainly have soon been at liberty. But M. Heger having heard of what was in agitation, sent for me the day after and pronounced with vehemence his decision that I could not leave. I could not at that time have persevered in my intentions without exciting him to anger; and promised to stay a little while longer.'*

And so what had to be done in the end was postponed: and the old hidden enmity between Charlotte and Madame Heger went on for another three months.

CHAPTER V

THE LEAVE-TAKING—
THE SCENE IN THE CLASS-ROOM—
CHARLOTTE LEAVES BRUSSELS

Two other events that we know must have happened within a few days of Charlotte's departure from Brussels, 2nd January 1844, are lit up by the emotions painted in *Villette.* We cannot doubt that these emotions were suffered by the woman of genius who describes them, because it is, not imagination, but remembrance, that has given these pages the magical touch of life, the 'vibration' that translates words 'into feelings,' so that we are not readers, but witnesses, of what this tormented heart endures.

Anguish of suspense; heart-sickness of hope deferred; despair, following on repeated disappointment; rage and indignation at the cruelty and injustice of this outrage done to a Love, that has wronged no one, robbed no one, that has no desire to inflict injury on others; yet that is refused the right that even the condemned criminal is *not* refused,—to bid farewell to what he holds most dear on earth before he goes forth to execution—all these feelings are painted in the wonderful pages, where the circumstances of the story nevertheless are legendary, and belong to the parable of Lucy Snowe: but where the sufferings Lucy endures on the eve of her separation from Paul Emanuel were facts stored up in the experiences of Charlotte Brontë.

Like the incident of Lucy Snowe's 'Confession,' the passages that in *Villette* describe the efforts made by Madame Beck and the Jesuit, Père Silas, to prevent Paul Emanuel from bidding

Lucy farewell, before he starts for his voyage to Basseterres in Guadeloupe, are pages from the spiritual life of Charlotte Brontë—taken out of their proper frame of circumstances, and altered in some important details. But outside of these alterations, one recognises their truthfulness, in the vivid light they throw upon the facts told us in Charlotte's correspondence.

In the novel, Paul Emanuel is expected to visit the class-room at a certain hour and to take farewell of his pupils. In connection with the real events, it has to be remembered that Charlotte left Bruxelles on the 2nd January, that is to say, in a period when, from Christmas day to perhaps the 7th January, there would be holidays, and the Bruxelles pupils would have gone to their homes. It is probable then that the English teacher, before the breaking-up, would have taken her farewell of her pupils in the class-rooms—this was the usual practice when a teacher was leaving for good—and that M. Heger, whom she hoped to have seen upon this occasion, would have been absent.

There would have been also a last lesson in class given by M. Heger before the breaking-up for these short Christmas holidays—the last lesson of his, that Charlotte, before she quitted the Pensionnat for ever, would have had the chance of attending. But, *like Madame Beck*, Madame Heger would have kept her English teacher employed in writing letters at her dictation, in her private sitting-room, whilst this class was going on. Like Lucy, Charlotte would have broken away at the end, when she heard the sound of moving forms, and shutting desks, proving the lesson ended. But here also Madame Heger would have followed her (even as Madame Beck followed Lucy Snowe)—have kept the under-mistress in the background, and then have taken possession of M. Heger, on the plea of some business matter demanding his attention.

Certainly also (it seems to me) we may believe in the incident of the scrap of paper, handed by one of the smallest girls in the school, to Charlotte, after these two exploits of Madame Heger's diplomacy, intended to avoid the danger—*and was not the danger real?*—of an emotional scene of leave-taking, that might thwart her endeavour to get Charlotte safely out of the house, without any 'inconvenient' revelations. M. Heger may, or may not, have been as ignorant of all that was going on between his wife and 'Mees Charlotte' as Madame Heger desired him to be. But it would have been entirely like him, whether he knew what was happening or not, to wish for an emotional leave-taking with his English pupil. M. Heger liked to foster a certain amount of sensibility in his relationships with his pupils—it did not amount to more than a taste for dramatic situations where he had an interesting part to play that gave his histrionic talents a good field of exercise. But the message warning Charlotte '*that he must see her at leisure, before she left, and talk with her at length*,' appears to me just the sort of message M. Heger would have sent. And more especially he would have acted thus if *in reality he had forgotten all about Charlotte's near time of departure* and then had suddenly remembered it, and that 'Mees' would feel hurt, and think he had behaved coldly to her. In this case he would have tried to put himself right and to persuade her that he had not forgotten at all, but had arranged a special opportunity for a long talk, etc. And Charlotte believing it all, upon the strength of this note, would have lingered on in his class-room, expecting M. Heger,—who never appeared.

M. HEGER AT SIXTY
(He was born in 1809: hence thirty-four in 1843, when Charlotte bade him farewell)

It seems to me that, whilst it is *possible* that Madame Heger *may* have prevented her husband from keeping the appointment, it is also quite *possible* that M. Heger may have again forgotten all about it? That would have been like him too,—as I shall show by and by.

But what I believe to have *certainly happened is that the scene between Madame Heger and Charlotte took place just as the authoress of 'Villette' described.* That interview wears, to my mind, the stamp of truth.

The last day broke. Now would he visit us. Now would he come and speak his farewell, or he would vanish mute, and be seen by us nevermore.

This alternative seemed to be present in the mind of not a living creature in that school. All rose at the usual hour; all breakfasted as usual; all, without reference to, or apparent thought of, their late professor, betook themselves with wonted phlegm to their ordinary duties.

So oblivious was the house, so tame, so trained its proceedings, so inexpectant its aspect, I scarce knew how to breathe in an atmosphere thus stagnant, thus smothering. Would no one lend me a voice? Had no one a wish, no one a word, no one a prayer to which I could say Amen?

I had seen them unanimous in demand for the merest trifle—a treat, a holiday, a lesson's remission; they could not, they*would* not now band to besiege Madame Beck, and insist on a last interview with a master who had certainly been loved, at least by some—loved as *they* could love; but, oh! what *is* the love of the multitude?

I knew where he lived; I knew where he was to be heard of or communicated with. The distance was scarce a stone's-throw. Had it been in the next room, unsummoned I could make no use of my knowledge. To follow, to seek out, to remind, to recall—for these things I had no faculty.

M. Emanuel might have passed within reach of my arm. Had he passed silent and unnoticing, silent and stirless should I have suffered him to go by.

Morning wasted. Afternoon came, and I thought all was over. My heart trembled in its place. My blood was troubled in its current. I was quite sick, and hardly knew how to keep at my post or do my work. Yet the little world round me plodded on indifferent; all seemed jocund, free of care, or fear, or thought. The very pupils who, seven days since, had wept hysterically at a startling piece of news, appeared quite to have forgotten the news, its import, and their emotion.

A little before five o'clock, the hour of dismissal, Madame Beck sent for me to her chamber, to read over and translate some English letter she had received, and to write for her the answer. Before settling to this work, I observed that she softly closed the two doors of her chamber; she even shut and fastened the casement, though it was a hot day, and free circulation of air was usually regarded by her as indispensable. Why this precaution? A keen suspicion, an almost fierce distrust, suggested such question. Did she want to exclude sound? What sound?

I listened as I had never listened before; I listened like the evening and winter wolf, snuffing the snow, scenting prey, and hearing far off the traveller's tramp. Yet I could both listen and write. About the middle of the letter I heard what checked my pen—a tread in the vestibule. No door-bell had rung; Rosine—acting doubtless by orders—had anticipated such reveille. Madame saw me halt. She coughed, made a bustle, spoke louder. The tread had passed on to the *classes*.

'Proceed,' said Madame; but my hand was fettered, my ear enchained, my thoughts were carried off captive.

The *classes* formed another building; the hall parted them from the dwelling-house. Despite distance and partition, I heard the sudden stir of numbers, a whole division rising at once.

'They are putting away work,' said madame.

It was indeed the hour to put away work, but why that sudden hush, that instant quell of the tumult?

'Wait, madam; I will see what it is.'

And I put down my pen and left her. Left her? No. She would not be left. Powerless to detain me, she rose and followed, close as my shadow. I turned on the last step of the stair.

'Are you coming too?' I asked.

'Yes,' she said, meeting my glance with a peculiar aspect—a look clouded, yet resolute. We proceeded then, not together, but she walked in my steps.

He was come. Entering the first *classe*, I saw him. There once more appeared the form most familiar. I doubt not they had tried to keep him away, but he was come.

The girls stood in a semicircle; he was passing round, giving his farewells, pressing each hand, touching with his lips each cheek. This last ceremony foreign custom permitted at such a parting—so solemn, to last so long.

I felt it hard that Madame Beck should dog me thus, following and watching me close. My neck and shoulder shrank in fever under her breath; I became terribly goaded.

He was approaching; the semicircle was almost travelled round; he came to the last pupil; he turned. But Madame was before me; she had stepped out suddenly; she seemed to magnify her proportions and amplify her drapery; she eclipsed me; I was hid. She knew my weakness and deficiency; she could calculate the degree of moral paralysis, the total default of self-assertion, with which, in a crisis, I could be struck. She hastened to her kinsman, she broke upon him volubly, she mastered his attention, she hurried him to the door—the glass door opening on the garden. I think he looked round. Could I but have caught his eye, courage, I think, would have rushed in to aid feeling, and there would have been a charge, and, perhaps, a rescue; but already the room was all confusion, the semicircle broken into groups, my figure was lost among thirty more conspicuous. Madame had her will. Yes, she got him away, and he had not seen me. He thought me absent. Five o'clock struck, the loud dismissal bell rang, the school separated, the room emptied.

There seems, to my memory, an entire darkness and distraction in some certain minutes I then passed alone—a grief inexpressible over a loss unendurable. *What* should I do—oh! *what* should I do—when all my life's hope was thus torn by the roots out of my riven, outraged heart?

What I *should* have done I know not, when a little child—the least child in the school—broke with its simplicity and its unconsciousness into the raging yet silent centre of that inward conflict.

'Mademoiselle,' lisped the treble voice, 'I am to give you that. M. Paul said I was to seek you all over the house, from the *grenier* to the cellar, and when I found you to give you that.'

And the child delivered a note. The little dove dropped

on my knee, its olive leaf plucked off. I found neither address nor name, only these words,—

'It was not my intention to take leave of you when I said good-bye to the rest, but I hoped to see you in *classe*. I was disappointed. The interview is deferred. Be ready for me. Ere I sail, I must see you at leisure, and speak with you at length. Be ready. My moments are numbered, and, just now, monopolized; besides, I have a private business on hand which I will not share with any, nor communicate, even to you.—Paul.'

'Be ready!' Then it must be this evening. Was he not to go on the morrow? Yes; of that point I was certain. I had seen the date of his vessel's departure advertised. Oh! *I* would be ready. But could that longed-for meeting really be achieved? The time was so short, the schemers seemed so watchful, so active, so hostile. The way of access appeared strait as a gully, deep as a chasm; Apollyon straddled across it, breathing flames. Could my Greatheart overcome? Could my guide reach me?

Who might tell? Yet I began to take some courage, some comfort. It seemed to me that I felt a pulse of his heart beating yet true to the whole throb of mine.

I waited my champion. Apollyon came trailing his hell behind him. I think if eternity held torment, its form would not be fiery rack, nor its nature despair. I think that on a certain day amongst those days which never dawned, and will not set, an angel entered Hades, stood, shone, smiled, delivered a prophecy of conditional pardon, kindled a doubtful hope of bliss to come, not now, but at a day and hour unlooked for, revealed in his own glory and grandeur the height and compass of his promise—spoke thus, then towering, became a star, and vanished into his own heaven. His legacy was suspense—a worse born than despair.

All that evening I waited, trusting in the dove-sent olive leaf, yet in the midst of my trust terribly fearing. My fear pressed heavy. Cold and peculiar, I knew it for the partner of a rarely-belied presentiment. The first hours seemed long and slow; in spirit I clung to the flying skirts of the last. They passed like drift cloud—like the rack scudding before a storm.

Prayers were over; it was bed-time; my co-inmates were all retired. I still remained in the gloomy first *classe*, forgetting, or at least disregarding, rules I had never forgotten or disregarded before.

How long I paced that *classe*, I cannot tell; I must have been afoot many hours. Mechanically had I moved aside benches and desks, and had made for myself a path down its length. There I walked, and there, when certain that the whole household were abed and quite out of hearing, there I at last wept. Reliant on night, confiding in solitude, I kept my tears sealed, my sobs chained, no longer. They heaved my heart; they tore their way. In this house, what grief could be sacred!

Soon after eleven o'clock—a very late hour in the Rue Fossette—the door unclosed, quietly, but not stealthily; a lamp's flame invaded the moonlight. Madame Beck entered, with the same composed air as if coming on an ordinary occasion, at an ordinary season. Instead of at once addressing me, she went to her desk, took her keys, and seemed to seek something. She loitered over this feigned search long, too long. She was calm, too calm. My mood scarce endured the pretence. Driven beyond common rage, two hours since I had left behind me wonted respects and fears. Led by a touch and ruled by a word under usual circumstances, no yoke could now be borne, no curb obeyed.

'It is more than time for retirement,' said madame. 'The rule of the house has already been transgressed too long.'

Madame met no answer. I did not check my walk. When she came in my way I put her out of it.

'Let me persuade you to calm, Meess; let me lead you to your chamber,' said she, trying to speak softly.

'No!' I said. 'Neither you nor another shall persuade or lead me.'

'Your bed shall be warmed. Goton is sitting up still. She shall make you comfortable. She shall give you a sedative.'

'Madame,' I broke out, 'you are a sensualist. Under all your serenity, your peace, and your decorum, you are an undenied sensualist. Make your own bed warm and soft; take sedatives and meats, and drinks spiced and sweet, as much as you will. If you have any sorrow or disappointment (and perhaps you have—nay, I *know* you have) seek your own palliatives in your own chosen resources. Leave me, however. *Leave me*, I say!'

'I must send another to watch you, Meess; I must send Goton.'

'I forbid it. Let me alone. Keep your hand off me, and my life, and my troubles. O madame! in *your* hand there is both chill and poison. You envenom and you paralyse.'

'What have I done, Meess? You must not marry Paul. He cannot marry.'

'Dog in the manger!' I said, for I knew she secretly wanted him, and had always wanted him. She called him 'insupportable'; she railed at him for a 'devot.' She did not love; but she wanted to marry that she might bind him to her interest. Deep into some of madame's secrets I had entered, I know not how—by an intuition or an inspiration which came to me, I know not whence. In the course of living with her, too, I had slowly learned that, unless with an inferior, she must ever be a rival. She was *my* rival, heart and soul, though secretly, under the smoothest bearing, and utterly unknown to all save her and myself.

Two minutes I stood over madame, feeling that the whole woman was in my power, because in some moods, such as the present, in some stimulated states of perception, like that of this instant, her habitual disguise, her mask, and her domino were to me a mere network reticulated with holes; and I saw underneath a being heartless, self-indulgent, and ignoble. She quietly retreated from me. Meek and self-possessed, though very uneasy, she said, 'If I would not be persuaded to take rest, she must reluctantly leave me.' Which she did incontinent, perhaps even more glad to get away than I was to see her vanish.

This was the sole flash-eliciting, truth-extorting rencontre which ever occurred between me and Madame Beck; this short night scene was never repeated. It did not one whit change her manner to me. I do not know that she revenged it. I do not know that she hated me the worse for my fell candour. I think she bucklered herself with the secret philosophy of her strong mind, and resolved to forget what it irked her to remember. I know that to the end of

> our mutual lives there occurred no repetition of, no allusion to, that fiery passage.

Is it possible to doubt that this 'fiery passage,'—or one strangely like it—went to the building up of the impressions and emotions that transformed the early memories of Madame Heger, of whom Charlotte once spoke so kindly in her letters, as a generous friend who had offered her a post in her school more from a kind wish to help her than from selfish motives?

We have another scene of which again, it seems to me, we cannot doubt the autobiographical reality. If one need proof of this, it may be found in the admirable criticism of *Villette* by Mrs. Humphry Ward, who judges the book exclusively as the author's *literary masterpiece.* In this masterpiece, Mrs. Humphry Ward finds one notable flaw:—*it is this very passage*—which the critic affirms (and no doubt she is quite right) does not strike her as a convincing nor even as a credible account of the sentiments or behaviour that could have belonged to Lucy Snowe, the heroine in *Villette.* 'Lucy Snowe,' this critic complains, 'could never have broken down, never have appealed for mercy, never have cried "*My heart will break*" before her treacherous rival Madame Beck in Paul Emanuel's presence! A reader by virtue of the very force of the effect produced upon him by the whole creation has a right to protest, incredible. No woman, least of all Lucy Snowe, could have so understood her own cause, could have so fought her own battle.'

I am ready to accept this sentence as an entirely authoritative literary sentence, first of all on account of the unquestionable claims of the critic who utters it to pronounce judgment on these matters; and then because I feel myself entirely unable, by reason of my personal acquaintanceships with the real people dressed up in strange disguises in this book, and placed in positions that the real people never occupied, to judge this particular novel, *Villette*, from a purely literary standpoint. Thus I agree that Mrs. Humphry Ward is right when she says that Lucy Snowe, *by virtue of the very force of the effect produced by this creation*, could not have said, '*My heart will break,' before her treacherous rival Madame Beck, in Paul Emanuel's presence.* I admit this, because Lucy Snowe, Madame Beck and Paul Emanuel, if not absolutely 'creations,' in the sense of being imaginary characters, are nevertheless different people from Charlotte Brontë, Madame Heger and Monsieur Heger, and their relationships to each other are different. Thus, in the novel Lucy Snowe is not only in love with Paul Emanuel, but she has a perfect right to be in love with him, not only because he is unmarried, but also because he has given her very good reason to believe he is in love with her: and Madame Beck has no sort of right to interfere with the lover of her English governess, and her cousin the Professor; and all her schemes to keep these two sympathetic creatures apart are absolutely unjustifiable, and the results of jealousy and selfishness. In other words, Lucy has the *beau rôle* in the piece,—she has no reason to say, 'My heart will break,' because Madame Beck intrudes upon her interview with Paul Emanuel.

But Charlotte had not the *beau rôle*, but the tragic one, in the real drama. The Directress, who stands between her and the beloved Professor, is not her rival, but the Professor's wife. And the *beau rôle*, in the sense of having the right to stand in the way, and also in being the woman preferred by the man whom both women love, is Madame Heger's in every way, for Madame Heger is charming to look at, and Charlotte plain. Therefore it is not in the least incredible, but it seems so natural as to be almost inevitably true, that when in the very moment that poor Charlotte has obtained, after so much suspense and waiting, and as the result of a heaven-sent accident, the almost despaired of chance of a personal interview with her loved Professor, before she loses sight of him, perhaps for ever, and when in this moment, and just when he has taken her hand in his,... Madame Heger enters, and thrusts herself between them, and commands her husband, '*Come, Constantin*,' and Charlotte believes he will obey, it seems to me so eminently credible as to be almost inevitably true, that what Charlotte describes happened, and that *then*, in dread of this new frustration of the hope so long deferred, an anguish that 'defied suppression' rang out in the cry 'My heart will break!' Put oneself in Charlotte's place, and it seems to me the emotion startled to expression by this new shock, expresses just what one knows she felt. And, therefore, I find it myself impossible to doubt that this account is literally true, and may and should be studied in the light of the assurance that we have here the faithful description of what really took place, upon the very day, perhaps, when Charlotte left Bruxelles.

Let us leave Lucy Snowe's love-story on one side, and judge this page as one torn out of Charlotte's life—and then decide whether it rings true.

> Shall I yet see him before he goes? Will he bear me in mind? Does he purpose to come? Will this day—will the next hour bring him? or must I again essay that corroding pain of long attent, that rude agony of rupture at the close, that mute, mortal wrench, which, in at once uprooting hope and doubt, shakes life, while the hand that does the violence cannot be caressed to pity, because absence interposes her barrier.
>
> It was the *Feast of the Assumption*[1]; no school was held. The boarders and teachers, after attending mass in the morning, were gone a long walk into the country to take their *goûter*, or afternoon meal, at some farmhouse. I did not go with them, for now but two days remained ere the *Paul et Virginie* must sail, and I was clinging to my last chance, as the living waif of a wreck clings to his last raft or cable.
>
> There was some joiner-work to do in the first *classe*, some bench or desk to repair. Holidays were often turned to account for the performance of these operations, which

could not be executed when the rooms were filled with pupils. As I sat solitary, purposing to adjourn to the garden and leave the coast clear, but too listless to fulfil my own intent, I heard the workmen coming.

Foreign artisans and servants do everything by couples. I believe it would take two Labassecourian carpenters to drive a nail. While tying on my bonnet, which had hitherto hung by its ribbons from my idle hand, I vaguely and momentarily wondered to hear the step of but one *ouvrier*. I noted, too—as captives in dungeons find sometimes dreary leisure to note the merest trifles—that this man wore shoes, and not sabots. I concluded that it must be the master-carpenter coming to inspect before he sent his journeymen. I threw round me my scarf. He advanced; he opened the door. My back was towards it. I felt a little thrill, a curious sensation, too quick and transient to be analysed. I turned, I stood in the supposed master-artisan's presence. Looking towards the doorway I saw it filled with a figure, and my eyes printed upon my brain the picture of M. Paul.

Hundreds of the prayers with which we weary Heaven bring to the suppliant no fulfilment. Once haply in life one golden gift falls prone in the lap—one boon full and bright, perfect from Fruition's mint.

M. Emanuel wore the dress in which he probably purposed to travel—a surtout, guarded with velvet. I thought him prepared for instant departure, and yet I had understood that two days were yet to run before the ship sailed. He looked well and cheerful. He looked kind and benign. He came in with eagerness; he was close to me in one second; he was all amity. It might be his bridegroom-mood which thus brightened him. Whatever the cause, I could not meet his sunshine with cloud. If this were my last moment with him, I would not waste it in forced, unnatural distance. I loved him well—too well not to smite out of my path even Jealousy herself, when she would have obstructed a kind farewell. A cordial word from his lips, or a gentle look from his eyes, would do me good for all the span of life that remained to me. It would be comfort in the last strait of loneliness. I would take it—I would taste the elixir, and pride should not spill the cup.

The interview would be short, of course. He would say to me just what he had said to each of the assembled pupils. He would take and hold my hand two minutes. He would touch my cheek with his lips for the first, last, only time, and then—no more. Then, indeed, the final parting, then the wide separation, the great gulf I could not pass to go to him, across which, haply, he would not glance to remember me.

He took my hand in one of his; with the other he put back my bonnet. He looked into my face, his luminous smile went out, his lips expressed something almost like the wordless language of a mother who finds a child greatly and unexpectedly changed, broken with illness, or worn out by want. A check supervened.

'Paul, Paul!' said a woman's hurried voice behind—'Paul, come into the *salon*. I have yet a great many things to say to you—conversation for the whole day—and so has Victor; and Josef is here. Come, Paul—come to your friends.'

Madame Beck, brought to the spot by vigilance or an inscrutable instinct, pressed so near she almost thrust herself between me and M. Emanuel. 'Come, Paul!' she reiterated, her eye grazing me with its hard ray like a steel stylet.

She pushed against her kinsman. I thought he receded; I thought he would go. Pierced deeper than I could endure, made now to feel what defied suppression, I cried,—

'My heart will break!'

What I felt seemed literal heartbreak; but the seal of another fountain yielded under the strain. One breath from M. Paul, the whisper, 'Trust me!' lifted a load, opened an outlet. With many a deep sob, with thrilling, with icy shiver, with strong trembling, and yet with relief, I wept.

'Leave her to me; it is a crisis. I will give her a cordial, and it will pass,' said the calm Madame Beck.

To be left to her and her cordial seemed to me something like being left to the poisoner and her bowl. When M. Paul answered deeply, harshly, and briefly, 'Laissez-moi!' in the grim sound I felt a music strange, strong, but life-giving.

'Laissez-moi!' he repeated, his nostrils opening, and his facial muscles all quivering as he spoke.

'But this will never do,' said madame with sternness.

More sternly rejoined her kinsman,—

'Sortez d'ici!'

'I will send for Père Silas; on the spot I will send for him,' she threatened pertinaciously.

'Femme!' cried the professor, not now in his deep tones, but in his highest and most excited key—'femme! sortez à l'instant!'

He was roused, and I loved him in his wrath with a passion beyond what I had yet felt.

'What you do is wrong,' pursued madame; 'it is an act characteristic of men of your unreliable, imaginative temperament—a step impulsive, injudicious, inconsistent—a proceeding vexatious, and not estimable in the view of persons of steadier and more resolute character.'

'You know not what I have of steady and resolute in me,' said he, 'but you shall see; the event shall teach you. Modeste,' he continued, less fiercely, 'be gentle, be pitying, be a woman. Look at this poor face, and relent. You know I am your friend and the friend of your friends; in spite of your taunts you well and deeply know I may be trusted. Of sacrificing myself I made no difficulty, but my heart is pained by what I see. It *must* have and give solace. *Leave me!*'

This time, in the '*leave me*' there was an intonation so bitter and so imperative, I wondered that even Madame Beck herself could for one moment delay obedience. But she stood firm; she gazed upon him dauntless; she met his eyes, forbidding and fixed as stone. She was opening her lips to retort. I saw over all M. Paul's face a quick rising light and fire. I can hardly tell how he managed the movement. It did not seem violent; it kept the form of courtesy. He gave his hand; it scarce touched her, I thought; she ran, she whirled from the room; she was gone, and the door shut, in one second.

The flash of passion was all over very soon. He smiled as he told me to wipe my eyes; he waited quietly till I was calm, dropping from time to time a stilling, solacing word. Ere long I sat beside him once more myself—reassured, not desperate, nor yet desolate; not friendless, not hopeless, not sick of life and seeking death.

'It made you very sad, then, to lose your friend?' said he.

'It kills me to be forgotten, monsieur,' I said. 'All these weary days I have not heard from you one word, and I was crushed with the possibility, growing to certainty, that you would depart without saying farewell.'

'Must I tell you what I told Modeste Beck—that you do not know me? Must I show and teach you my character? You *will*have proof that I can be a firm friend? Without clear proof this hand will not lie still in mine, it will not trust my shoulder as a safe stay? Good. The proof is ready. I come to justify myself.'

'Say anything, teach anything, prove anything, monsieur; I can listen now.'

After this, in *Villette*, the story drifts away from the real experience of Charlotte herself, not only in the circumstances related, but even in the emotions pictured, now painted, not from what she has felt herself, but from what she imagines for her heroine, that other happier self, lifted up into the heaven of romance, who, assured of Paul Emanuel's love, and his betrothed, waits and works in the school where he has appointed her Directress; in patient expectation of his return,—*that never comes to pass!* For (why or wherefore, no literary critic of *Villette* who measures the book by simply artistic standards can find any reason to explain) Charlotte won't let Lucy Snowe, the heroine, who is her other self, find happiness at last with Paul Emanuel: or even find him again, after that cruel separation, all due to the wicked craft and selfish jealousy of Madame Beck. Destiny interferes; a storm; a shipwreck—one is not told *what* has happened: one is made to hear wailing winds and moaning ocean, that is all; we know nothing further than this: *Lucy Snowe waited and hoped; hoped and waited; but Paul Emanuel never came back.*

But, at any rate, before he sailed on that last fatal voyage, all misunderstandings, all doubts had been swept away. He had driven Madame Beck from the room, and shown her his contempt and indignation. He had, with tenderness and passion, declared his love for Lucy; and had asked her to be his wife. This is what had followed after those scenes between Lucy and Madame Beck in the late night scene in the class-rooms and between Lucy and Paul Emanuel, when Madame Beck is put out of the room by Paul Emanuel, who insists upon saying good-bye to Lucy.

All that we know of what followed these scenes, enacted under different circumstances, in Charlotte's life, must be gathered, not by a quite literal acceptance, but by an intelligent and impartial weighing, of her statements, contained in a letter written on the 23rd January 1844, three weeks after her return to Haworth.

'I suffered much before I left Brussels. I think, however long I live, I shall not forget what the parting with M. Heger cost me: it grieved me so much to grieve him, who had been so true, kind and disinterested a friend. At parting, he gave me a kind of diploma certifying my abilities as a teacher sealed with the seal of the Athenée Royal of which he is a professor.... I do not know whether you feel as I do, but there are times when it appears to me as if all my ideas and feelings, except a few friendships and affections, are changed from what they used to be. Something in me which used to be enthusiasm is tamed down and broken. I no longer regard myself as young—indeed I shall soon be twenty-eight—and it seems as if I ought to be working and having the rough realities of the world as other people do.'[2]

[1]New Year's Day, perhaps? Charlotte left Bruxelles 2nd January 1843.

[2]*Life*, p. 273.

CHAPTER VI

THE LOVE-LETTERS OF A ROMANTIC

[1]

Taking up the study of Charlotte's letters written to M. Heger after her return to Haworth, and reading them in the light of what we know of the circumstances and emotions that have formed the feelings, and decided the tone and attitude of the writer, what do we find to be the sentiment they reveal to us?

Is it the 'enthusiasm for a great man,' and the desire (for the sake of vanity, or of amusement) to keep up a correspondence with him?

Or is it the intellectual need of this teacher's instructions and advice, as a means of mental improvement?

Or is it the want of a companion to exchange ideas with, who is a brighter and more cultivated being than the Nusseys, Taylors, Woolers, and the others?

Or is it the pleasure of having a man friend, in the case of a woman who is neither pretty, nor young, nor silly, enough to indulge in an ordinary flirtation?

Or is it none amongst these several forms of desire, or want, that seeks its own good?

Is it love?—a love so exalted, so passionate, so personal, so distinct from any other instinct or interest, physical, social or intellectual, that this sentiment stands out, in the order of human feelings, as honourable not only to the heart that feels it, but to human nature: so that brought into touch with it, one's own heart is uplifted above the common world, and gladdened '*by the sense,*' as Byron said,[2] '*of the existence of Love in its most extended and sublime capacity and of our own participation of its good and of its glory.*[3]

My contention is that it *is* this romantic Love that reveals itself in Charlotte's letters to M. Heger. And for this reason, I agree with Mr. Clement Shorter that they put her upon a higher pedestal than ever. For to have a heart capable of this great and glorious, albeit often tragical, romantic Love, that 'seeketh not its own,' and compared with which all other sorts of love, that *do* seek their own, are as sounding brass and a tinkling cymbal is, *independently of deeds or works*, greatly to serve mankind. For it is to stand as a witness, amongst the meannesses of mortal and worldly things, to the existence of Something personal and immortal in the soul and heart of man, helping him '*to gild his dross thereby.*'[4] Something sovereign, that, quite independently of forms of belief, or fashions of opinion, '*rules by every school, till love and longing die.*' Something indestructible, confined to no epoch, ancient, mediæval or modern, but, '*that was, or yet the lights were set, a whisper in the void; that will be sung in planets young when this is clean destroyed.*' In other words, I esteem human nature honoured in Charlotte Brontë, and Charlotte Brontë honoured in these Letters, *because they are love-letters of a rare and wonderful sort amongst the most beautiful, although they are the most sad ever written.* If they were *not* love-letters, but expressed the enthusiasm of a woman wanting comradeship with a great man, I should esteem them discreditable to any hero-worshipper. Because one should not pester one's hero with letters, nor conceive the conceit of comradeship with an object of worship. And it is not true that Charlotte's letters to Thackeray, George Henry Lewes and other men of letters after she became famous, had the same character as these love-letters written to M. Heger before her name was known; because in her letters to different celebrated writers, Charlotte talked about books or the criticism of books. But to M. Heger she throws open the secret chamber of her heart: she pours out its treasures of passionate feelings (as pure as they were passionate) at the feet of the man she loves; all she asks for from him in return is not to reprove her, nor refuse the offering; not to withdraw himself from her life altogether. To let her hear from him sometimes: not to leave her utterly alone, in the darkness, without any knowledge of what good or evil may befall one so dear to her.

Unfortunately we do not possess the first Letters of this correspondence. The four Letters given by Dr. Paul Heger to the British Museum all belong to a period when the Professor, who had answered (one does not know precisely in what way) Charlotte's first epistles, had left off replying to her; and the consistent motive of these four appeals is for some tidings of him, some proof that the 'estrangement from her Master,' to which she says she will never 'voluntarily' consent, has not, in spite of her own unaltered devotion, irrevocably taken place.

'Tell me about anything you like, my Master,' she writes, 'only tell me something! No doubt, to write to a former under-mistress (no, I will not remember my employment as under-mistress, I refuse to recall it), but to write to an old pupil, cannot be, for you, an interesting occupation. I realise this; but for *me*, it is life. Your last letter served to keep me alive, to nourish me during six months. Now I must have another one; and you will give me one. Not because you bear me friendship (you cannot bear me much!), but because you have a compassionate soul, and because you would not condemn any one to slow suffering, simply to spare yourself a few moments of fatigue! To forbid me to write to you, to refuse to reply to me, would be to tear from me the only joy that I have in the world; to deprive me of my last privilege, a privilege which I will never *voluntarily* renounce. Believe me, my Master! by writing to me, you do a good action—so long as I can believe you are not angry with me, so long as the hope is left me of news of you, I can be tranquil, and not too sad. But when a gloomy and prolonged silence warns me of the estrangement from me of my Master, when from day to day I expect a letter, and when, day after day, comes disappointment, to plunge me in overwhelming grief; and when the sweet and dear consolation of seeing your handwriting, of reading your counsels, fades from me like a vain vision,—then fever attacks me, appetite and sleep fail: I feel that life wastes away.'[5]

This passage is quoted from the Letter dated by Charlotte 18*th November*, without any indication of the year. Mr. Spielmann (who is responsible for the order given the Letters in the *Times*) esteems this one to be the last of the series; that is to say, to have been written ten months after the Letter dated by Charlotte 8 January, supposed by him to belong to the year 1845. With Dr. Paul Heger, I believe, on the contrary, that the Letter of the 18th November is the first of the series: and that it belongs to the year 1844; that is to say, was written ten months after Charlotte's return to England. This opinion seems to me established by the contents of the Letter, and by the account it gives of the conditions of affairs at Haworth, which were those that we find (if we consult Mrs. Gaskell's *Life of Charlotte Brontë*) did prevail in November 1844, but not in November 1845, and still less in November 1846.

> My father (she writes) is in good health, but his eyesight is all but gone; he can no longer either read or write: and yet the doctors advise waiting some months longer before attempting any operation. This winter will be for him one long night. He rarely complains: and I admire his patience. If Providence has the same calamity in reserve for me, may it grant me the same patience to endure it. It seems to me, Monsieur, that what is most bitter in severe physical afflictions, is that they compel us to share our sufferings with those who surround us. One can hide the maladies of the soul; but those that attack the body and enfeeble our faculties cannot be hidden. My father now allows me to read to and to write for him. He shows much more confidence in me than he has ever done before; and this is a great consolation to me.

Charlotte's account in this Letter of her father's patient resignation and increased confidence in her under the trial, to a man of his independent and somewhat domineering temper, of compulsory reliance on the assistance of a daughter from whom he had exacted complete submission heretofore and from her childhood upwards, is confirmed in Mrs. Gaskell's biography by the testimony of other letters belonging to the first year of her return from Belgium. But by November 1845 Mr. Brontë's philosophy, before his own unmerited misfortune, had been troubled and transformed into acute misery and anxious forebodings by the downfall, both moral and physical, of his favourite amongst his children, Bramwell, the unhappy son—the only one—in this family of gifted daughters, whose perversion seems also to have had something of the irresponsibility of genius about it. Writing on the 4th November 1845 to Ellen Nussey,[6] Charlotte says:—

> I hoped to be able to ask you to come to Haworth. It almost seemed as if Bramwell had a chance of getting employment; and I waited to know the results of his efforts, in order to say 'Dear Ellen, come and see us.' But the place is given to another person. Bramwell still remains at home, and whilst *he* is here, *you* shall not come.'

> November 1844, but not in November 1845,

Here is Mrs. Gaskell's account of Mr. Brontë's experiences in this period, that are not to be reconciled with the account given of his good health and philosophical patience and resignation to dependence upon Charlotte given by her a year earlier:

> For the last three years of his life, Bramwell took opium habitually, by way of stunning conscience: he drank, moreover, whenever he could get the opportunity.... He slept in his father's room; and he would sometimes declare that ei-

> ther he or his father would be dead before the morning! The trembling sisters, sick with fright, would implore their father not to expose himself to this danger. But Mr. Brontë was no timid man; and perhaps he felt that he could possibly influence his son to some self-restraint more by showing trust in him than by showing fear. The sisters often listened for the report of a pistol in the dead of night, till watchful eye and hearkening ear grew heavy and dull with the perpetual strain upon their nerves. In the mornings, young Brontë would saunter out saying, with a drunkard's incontinence of speech, 'The poor old man and I have had a terrible night of it; he does his best, the poor old man, but it's all over with me.'

One may safely affirm that if Charlotte had been writing in November 1845 it would not have been only his patience under the trial of loss of sight that she would have found to admire in her father. In November 1846 Mr. Brontë had successfully undergone the operation for cataract that saved him from blindness: and Charlotte herself, ten months after the overwhelming evidence of her 'master's estrangement,' given in his silence after her Letter of the 8th January, had saved her own soul from the malady she had endured without sharing her sufferings with any one; and was already writing *Jane Eyre* ... so that the conclusion is surely forced upon us that the Letter of the 18th November belongs to the year 1844, and written ten months after her return to Haworth, 2nd January 1844, and represents the first, and not the last of these four Letters.

REDUCED FROM A DRAWING BY CHARLOTTE BRONTË OF ASHBURNHAM CHURCH SENT TO M. HEGER

The drawing showing the date 1846 was given to the author by Mlle. Louise Heger

It is important to establish this, because one has to read these Letters in their right order before one can understand the story they disclose of the long training in deferred hope, in expectation, crowned with disappointment, in vain pursuit of shadows that eluded her grasp, and of illusions that reveal themselves as forms of self-deceit only in the very hour when they have conquered belief; in other words, of the long training in personal suffering it took to create and fashion the genius of a writer whose magical gift was to be the power of transforming words into feelings.

Carrying through the examination of these documents by the rule that recognises the Letter of the 18th November as written ten months after Charlotte's return to England, we discover in the opening sentence the fact that the last letter Charlotte had received from her Professor must have been in May of this same year; that is to say, four months after the sentimental leave-taking with her Professor, which sent Charlotte home to England with illusions about the extent to which her own passionate grief at their separation was shared by M. Heger. By November these illusions have been dispelled; Charlotte understands perfectly now (although this does not make her any more just to Madame Heger) that the 'grief' of her 'Master,' that she had said she would 'never forget, never mind how long she might live,' was a very short-lived affair on his side; merely the transient regret of a teacher who will miss a favourite pupil from his class.

'*Que ne puis-je avoir pour vous juste autant d'amitié que vous avez pour moi,*' she writes to him, '*ni plus, ni moins? Je serais alors si tranquille, si libre: je pourrais garder le silence pendant six mois sans effort.*'

There is a note of bitterness in this. In what precedes it there is no bitterness, but we have one of the passages in these wonderful letters that seem to me to place them above all the other love-letters preserved in the world, as immortal records of the Romantic Love that honours human nature in the hearts that cherish it.

'The six months of silence are over: we are now at the 18th of November,' she writes:-

> I may, then, write to you, without breaking my promise. The summer and winter have seemed very long to me: in truth, it has cost me painful efforts to endure up to now the privation I have imposed upon myself. You, for your part, cannot understand this! But, Monsieur, try to imagine, for one moment, that one of your children is a hundred and sixty leagues away from you; and that you are condemned to remain for six months, without writing to him; without receiving any news from him; without hearing anything about him; without knowing how he is;—well, then you may be able to understand, perhaps, how hard is such an

obligation imposed upon me.

In connection with the opening phrase, we must recognise in it the confirmation of an assertion made in my article in the *Woman at Home* published twenty years before these Letters were published, but which had for its authority the information given me by Dr. Paul Heger upon the occasion of a conversation, when he very kindly talked over with me the questions connected with events in his parents' life that, inasmuch as they happened before his birth, he knew as family traditions chiefly—but still as traditions derived from the only authentic sources of information that exist: Dr. Paul Heger's theory was that until Charlotte had left Bruxelles and commenced to write to his father letters in a tone of exaltation that announced an exaggerated attachment, Monsieur Heger himself had never suspected the existence of any such sentiment; and that he, and Madame Heger (?)—were disposed to regard it as an attack of morbid regret for the more animated life she had led in Bruxelles, and the dulness of her home surroundings. And that, acting upon this supposition, they had thought it advisable (and this in Charlotte's own interests chiefly) to let her know that they were both of them distressed and displeased by the tone of her letters; and that if she wished to keep up the correspondence, she must become more reasonable and temperate in her way of expressing herself; and that, as the exchange of letters between busy people became onerous, there must be only two letters every year at intervals of six months. We find Charlotte acknowledging this condition, as one that she had accepted, but that she complained of as a great 'privation': and she then goes on to explain (as only one taught by romantic, that is to say by unselfish, and unsensual, love, that 'does not seek its own,' could explain it) in what this 'privation' consists.

Did any woman, neglected by the man she loves, ever discover a device, at once so passionate, and so poetically pure as Charlotte's, who makes the man who does not love her, but whom she knows is an adoring father, try to realise what she feels, so far away from him, and left without tidings *by asking him to picture what he would feel if separated by a hundred and sixty leagues from his little child, he were left without news of him?*

But now if we consult honestly our own impressions, does this letter reveal that '*it is no cause of grief to Charlotte that M. Heger is married*'? Is it true that *there 'is nothing in it that any enthusiastic woman might not write to a married man with a family who had been her teacher*'?

What the letter does reveal (thus it seems to me at least) is one supreme thing before all others: that the writer of it is past saving, by this time, from the destiny she prophesied for herself ten months ago in Bruxelles. '*My heart will break*,' Charlotte said then: when fate (in the garb of Madame Heger) thrust herself between her and her beloved Professor.

And now, touching and eloquent as it all is, what escape is there from the conclusion that the writer of this letter *must* break her heart?

What else can happen? Let us recognise her plight. Here one has an entirely honourable, passionately tender, tenderly passionate, very serious woman, her mind dominated (as she says herself) by one tyrannical fixed idea; let us rather say by one tragical passion; and who sees her own life, and her claims upon the man she loves through the medium of this tragical passion: *and who gives her life an impossible purpose; and who makes impossible claims.* They are very small claims, she pleads. And so they are, very small in comparison with what she gives, her whole life's devotion poured out at the feet of her 'Master,' from whom she only asks in return that he will not forbid her worship; that, now and again, he will give her the joy of seeing his handwriting, and of knowing that he is well. But small as these claims are, they are unreasonable:—'*to the last degree "inconvenient" and impossible*,' as Madame would have said,—in the particular case of this 'Master'; a married man and an attached husband with five children, the Director of a Pensionnat de Jeunes Filles who has need to be especially circumspect; and who cannot discreetly, nor even honourably, allow a former under-mistress to address him passionate, romantic love-letters, even every six months. Nor can this loyal husband and self-respecting Catholic and Professor undertake to appear to sanction this indiscretion, by keeping her informed of his health and welfare at regular intervals. So that, building her heart's desires upon false hopes, that, from day to day, wear themselves out in disappointment, and looking for consolation to things necessarily withdrawn; and that she pursues in vain like 'fading visions,'—how is our poor Charlotte to find any escape from the heart-break that is the natural term of the path along which this Love, that has become her destiny, leads her? No way of escape is there for Charlotte: not in heaven above, nor on the earth beneath, nor in the waters under the earth. For no miracle can give her love a happy ending; say that even a thunderbolt fell from heaven to remove Madame Heger,—it would be extremely unjust—but admit that a murderous miracle be granted—even so, it would not alter the fact that M. Heger is not in love with Charlotte. And no earthly scheme either can bridge the separation—wider than the 160 leagues between Yorkshire and Brussels—that now severs Charlotte, breaking her heart in Yorkshire, from her Master in literature, carrying on, as stormily and triumphantly as when she assisted at them, his lessons in the class-rooms in the Rue d'Isabelle: those memory-haunted class-rooms she will never see again; because although we find her in these Letters speaking of projects of earning money that she may return to Bruxelles, if only to see her professor once again, one knows that there would be Madame to count with; and even Monsieur Heger's obstinate neglect to reply to these appealing Letters does not indicate any answering wish on his side to see his former pupil again. Nor yet does there exist in the waters under the earth any pool of magical power of healing sufficient to soothe these bitter regrets and reproaches; nor any well deep enough to drown rebellious desires and memories: for Charlotte has too splendid a soul to think of suicide; or to quench anguish by drugs. So that one knows that Charlotte's fate is sealed: and that we must follow her through these last steps to the end, with pity and admiration and love for her—but still not with injustice to others. Because no one outside of herself, not Madame Heger, nor Monsieur Heger, is responsible for what has happened, and what is going to happen; but only the Love that has Charlotte's soul in thrall, the Love that 'seeketh not its own,'—romantic, or if it be preferred, Platonic Love; who as the wise woman, Diotima, told Socrates, is 'not a god, but an immortal spirit, who spans the gulf between heaven and earth, carrying to the gods the prayers of men, and to the earth the commands of the gods.' Love, who is 'the child of plenty and of poverty, often, like his mother, without house or home to cover him' (and who consequently is not highly esteemed by respectable householders). Love, the 'instinct of immortality in a mortal creature,' leading him amongst mortal conditions to where Charlotte is being led to,—the grave of hope,—*but not leaving hope there entombed, but raising it, not clogged with the pollution of mortality.*

All this, that the wise Diotima related, is a true parable of Charlotte Brontë. And the proof that Diotima was a good psychologist, and had based her opinions upon the study of facts, is found in the assertion that Love, although an immortal spirit, is *not a god.* Because a god sees clearly, and does not make mistakes: whereas Love, as every one knows, is often blind, and never very clear-sighted; and *is*liable to make mistakes, and to be unjust even: and to attribute his own errors to other people. Thus Charlotte, under the dominion of Love, was unjust, and made mistakes: she attributed to Madame Heger disappointments and misadventures and pangs, that were not of Madame Heger's preparation at all, but were simply the imprudences of this 'Child of plenty and poverty,' who inherits from both parents and is so often extravagant and houseless, and consequently in bad odour with householders and the worshippers of 'convenience,' because 'he has no home to cover him.' Charlotte should not have attributed, for instance, malevolence or jealousy or the cruel pleasure of tantalising and torturing her in Bruxelles to Madame Heger, simply because, as the Directress of a Pensionnat de Jeunes Filles and wife of M. Heger, she did not want to take in Romantic Love as a boarder; nor to permit this 'Child of plenty and poverty' to disorganise the well-balanced domestic and conjugal relationships between herself and M. Heger. In all this Madame Heger was not persecuting Charlotte, but protecting her own rights. And if we examine the circumstances even in the narrative of the scene in the class-room between the Directress and her English teacher, and the scene of the farewell interview between the Professor and his pupil, where the Directress of the Pensionnat is put out of the room because she objects to this sentimental leave-taking, we shall find that recognising the true relationships between these three people, if Madame Heger behaved exactly as Madame Beck is said to have done, then there is not any fault whatever to be found with Madame Heger. Nay, one does not see how she could have been more considerate. Another false impression of Charlotte's—that Madame Heger intercepted her letters, and that M. Heger did not answer because he did not receive them—has no evidence to support it. Nor is this all; there is undeniable proof that the letter we have just considered (*which M. Heger did not answer*) *was* received by him: and that he was not very much affected by the passionate homage of his worshipper. 'On the edge of this letter he has made some commonplace notes in pencil;—one of them is the name and address of a shoemaker,' Mr. Spielmann tells us.

There is a natural feeling of indignation against this masculine insensibility to a woman's tragical passion, even though one recognises that honour stood in the way of any responsive sentiment. But one must not forget M. Heger's special vocation and his daily occupations and preoccupations. Here you have a Professor of literature in a Pensionnat de Jeunes Filles who spends, week by week, several days in correcting and improving 'compositions' and exercises in 'style' of numberless schoolgirls, full of the eloquent sentimentality that belongs to young writers between the ages of fourteen and sixteen. Monsieur Heger had been Charlotte's master in literature, remember: and there is another fact to be realised also, one that upon the authority of my own knowledge of him, in the character of my own Professor, I am allowed to testify to: *he was before all things a born teacher, and one who saw the world as his class-room, and his fellow-creatures in the light of pupils.* Applying this knowledge of him to the criticism of what we know about his relations with Charlotte Brontë, we arrive at entirely different opinions to those formed by people who either see M. Heger through the medium of Charlotte's passion for him and as she painted him in *Villette*; or outside of any personal knowledge of him at all, as he appears to them judged in the light of the impression that he played with Charlotte's feelings: first of all encouraging by sentimental flattery her affection for him, and then, when he found that she had become inconveniently fond of him, behaving with cruel indifference. None of these decisions is based on a correct knowledge of M. Heger, nor of his true behaviour and character. The true M. Heger was not the Paul Emanuel who was *the lover of Lucy Snowe*, because he is very truthfully and admirably painted in the domineering but interesting, terror-striking but captivating, masterful and masterly Professor of literature, so full of talent, and fiery captivating ardour for beautiful thoughts nobly expressed. The real Professor was *not* tender-hearted; nor very tender in manner; nor even very pleasant and considerate; nor even kind, outside of his professorial character: and he had no sympathy whatever to spare for people who were not his pupils. And his sympathy for his pupils, *as his pupils*, led him to work upon their sympathies, as a way of inducing a frame of mind in them and an emotional state of feeling, rendering them susceptible to literary impressions, and putting them in key with himself, in this very fine enthusiasm of his, not only for enjoying literature himself, but for throwing open to others, and to young votaries especially, the worship of beautiful literature—as the record of the best that has been thought and said in the world.

But the very exclusive literary temperament of M. Heger left him rather cold-blooded than particularly warm-hearted, where his pupils' feelings interfered with their good style in writing; or good accent when speaking; or with their sense of the first importance of a warm appreciation of the beauties of literature. If one reversed directly the description of Charlotte Brontë herself, as a writer whose *words became feelings*, one might justly say of M. Heger that for him, feelings were chiefly good with reference to their effects upon words, and the creation of beautiful language—so that Charlotte's love-letters to him would be no more than the '*Devoirs de Style*' of a former pupil sent him for criticism. The shoemaker's address may have been jotted down by accident, when he was running his eye down the page? If the further notes signified by Mr. Spielmann on this page, where poor Charlotte's heart's Secret lay exposed and quivering, had been '*Bon—mais un peu trop d'exaltation—la Ponctuation n'est pas soignée*,' no one who knew M. Heger would blame him for *voluntary* unkindness. But upon this matter no more must be said at present: we have to return to Charlotte, and her Letters.

The second in the order in which I am studying them (that seems to me unmistakably indicated by the context) would have been written—if we take the year 1845 as the date—eight, instead of six, months after the one, dated November, that refers to a preceding letter in the May of the same year—when Charlotte would have accepted the obligation laid upon her not to write again for six months. This Letter, dated 24th July, indicates by the opening sentence, not that she is writing outside of the appointed time, but *outside of her turn*: that is to say, it shows that M. Heger had not answered her November Letter; that she had waited for his reply, but could not wait longer, and so wrote a second letter, before M. Heger's reply to the first. The custom shows us that poor Charlotte is uneasily conscious that her former one in November may have given offence. She apologises for it, as we shall see; and works hard to write with cheerfulness in a more temperate tone:—

> Ah, Monsieur! I know I once wrote you a letter that was not a reasonable one, because my heart was choked with grief; but I will not do it again! I will try not to be selfish; although I cannot but feel your letters the greatest happiness I know. I will wait patiently to receive one, until it pleases you, and it is convenient to write one. At the same time, I may write you a little letter from time to time; you authorised me to do that.

The effort she is putting upon herself in this Letter is evident. She has become reasonable; she does not reproach him for not writing, but only asks him to remember how much she desires it. She tells him of her plans, as she was recommended to do, instead of dwelling on her feelings. She humours and flatters his vanity and taste by her acknowledgment of all she owes him; and of her unfailing gratitude and wish to dedicate a book to him—she even sends a message to Madame!—

> *Please present to Madame the assurance of my esteem.* I fear that Maria, Louise and Claire will have forgotten me. Prospère and Victorine never knew me, but I remember all five of them, and especially Louise. There was so much character, so much naiveté expressed in her little face. Farewell, Monsieur—Your grateful pupil,
>
> C. Brontë.
>
> *July* 24.—I have not begged you to write to me soon, because I am afraid of troubling you, but you are too kind to forget how much I desire it. Yes! I do desire it so much. But that is enough. After all, do as you like, Monsieur, for if I received a letter from you and I thought you wrote it out of pity, it would hurt me very much.... Oh I shall certainly see you some day. It must come to pass. Because as soon as I earn any money, I shall go to Bruxelles—and I shall see

> you again, if only for a moment.

It is all of no avail! No answer does M. Heger vouchsafe. October comes round, and she writes again. This time she imagines that she has found a means of making her Letter reach its destination. In other words, she is convinced, or tries to be convinced, that it is all Madame Heger's fault again; she it is who will not allow her husband to receive Charlotte's Letters.

> *October* 24.—Monsieur—I am quite joyous to-day. A thing that has not often happened during the last two years.[7] The reason is that a gentleman amongst my friends is passing through Bruxelles, and he has offered to take charge of a letter for you, and to give this same letter into your hands; or else his sister will do this, so that I shall be quite certain that you receive it.

Now comes the final blow to this faithful worshipper. Up to this hour, she has hoped and waited, waited and hoped. But all this time there has been the suspicion of Madame Heger—that has kept alive in her the belief in M. Heger's friendship, who (perhaps?) writes, although his letters never arrive: who (perhaps?) never receives her letters, although whenever she dares, and even in defiance of the terms laid down for her, she writes him letters where the vibration of her passionate attachment is felt. Now, however, he *has* received her letter placed in his own hand. Had he written she would now have held in her turn the talisman of the beloved handwriting her eyes were weary with waiting to see again. But he remained obdurate and silent.

> Mr. Taylor has returned (she writes): I asked him if he had no letter for me. 'No: nothing.' Be patient, I told myself: soon his sister will return. Miss Taylor came back: 'I have nothing for you from Monsieur Heger,' she said; 'neither letter, nor any message.'

> Understanding only too well what this meant, I told myself just what I should have told any one else in the same circumstances: Resign yourself to what you cannot alter, and before all things do not grieve for a misfortune that you have not deserved. I would not allow myself to weep nor complain. But when one refuses to oneself the right to tears and lamentations in certain cases, one is a tyrant; and natural faculties revolt; so that one buys outward calm at the price of an inner conflict that cannot be subdued.
>
> Neither by day, nor by night can I find rest nor peace: even if I sleep, I have tormenting dreams, where I see you, always severe, gloomy, angry with me. Forgive me, Monsieur, if I am driven to take the course of writing to you once more. How can I endure my life, if I am forbidden to make any effort to alleviate my sufferings?

She continues in this piteous strain. She pleads with him not to reprove her again as she has been reproved before, for exaggeration, morbidness, sentimentality. She tells him all this may be true—she is not going to defend herself—but the case is as she states it. She *cannot* resign herself to the loss of her master's friendship without one last effort to preserve it.

> I submit to all the reproaches you may make against me; if my master withdraws his friendship from me entirely, I shall remain without hope; if he keeps a little for me (never mind though it be *very* little) I shall have some motive for living, for working.
>
> Monsieur (she continues), the poor do not need much to keep them alive; they ask only for the crumbs that fall from the rich man's table, but if these crumbs are refused them, *then* they die of hunger! For me too, I make no claim either to great affection from those I love; I should hardly

know how to understand an exclusive and perfect friendship, I have so little experience of it! But once upon a time, at Bruxelles, when I was your pupil, you *did* show me a little interest: and just this small amount of interest you gave me then, I hold to and I care for and prize, as I hold to and care for life itself....

... I will not re-read this letter, I must send it as it is written. And yet I know, by some secret instinct, that certain absolutely reasonable and cool-headed people reading it through will say:—'She appears to have gone mad.' By way of revenge on such judges, all I would wish them is that they too might endure, *for one day only*, the sufferings I have borne for eight months—then, one would see, if they too did not 'appear to have gone mad.'

One endures in silence whilst one has his strength to do it. But when this strength fails one, one speaks without weighing one's words. I wish Monsieur all happiness and prosperity.

Haworth, Bradford, Yorkshire, 8*th January*.

The Letter obtained no answer. And thus the end was reached. We now know where in Charlotte Brontë's life lay her experiences that formed her genius and made her the great Romantic—whose quality was that she saw all events and personages through the medium of one passion—the passion of a predestined tragical and unrequited love.

END OF PART I.

[1]I have to thank Mr. Clement Shorter, who has purchased the copyright of Charlotte Brontë's manuscripts, for his generous

permission to quote from these letters freely for the purposes of my criticism.—(F.M.)

[2]*Childe Harold*, note 9 to canto iii.

[3]The author of *Childe Harold* adds on this note as a comment upon what he has said of 'Love' as the inspiration of the greatest of all Romantics, J.-J. Rousseau:—

'His love was passion's essence—as a tree
On fire by lightning; with ethereal flame
Kindled he was, and blasted; for to be
Thus, and enamour'd, were in him the same.
But his was not the love of living dame,
Nor of the dead who rise upon our dreams,
But of Ideal beauty, which became
In him existence and o'erflowing teems
Along his burning page, distemper'd tho' it seems.

This breathed itself to life in Julie, this
Invested her with all that's wild and sweet;
This hallow'd too the memorable kiss
Which every morn his fever'd lip would greet,
From hers, who but with friendship his would meet:
But to that gentle touch, thro' brain and breast
Flash'd the thrill'd spirit's love-devouring heat;
In that absorbing sigh perchance more blest
Than vulgar minds may be with all they seek possest.'

[4]Rudyard Kipling.

[5]See Letter, 18 Nov. I am giving my own translation from the French of Charlotte's Letters in these extracts, not certainly on account of any dissatisfaction with Mr. Spielmann's English versions of them, but in order to avoid the risk of any infringement of Mr. Spielmann's copyright in his Introduction.

[6]Mrs. Gaskell's *Life, p.* 290.

[7]Charlotte had been a year and ten months in England in

October 1845. This phrase, however, proves that the Letter belongs to this year and not to 1844, and consequently that the Letter that follows it, January 8, is 1846.

PART II

SOME REMINISCENCES OF THE
REAL MONSIEUR AND MADAME HEGER

THIS SECOND PART IS
DEDICATED TO
MY BROTHER
THE LATE ABBÉ AUSTIN RICHARDSON
WHO DIED SUDDENLY, 20TH AUG. 1913

Dearest, before you went away
And left me here behind you,
How often would you talk to me,
And I, too, would remind you
Of stories in this book retold,
That for us two could ne'er grow old;
Of scenes that we could live through yet,
Just you and I,—and not forget:
And now I feel, since you are gone,
I wrote this book for you alone.

CHAPTER I

THE HISTORICAL DIFFICULTY: TO DISENTANGLE FACT FROM FICTION

The purpose of the First Part of this study was to show that with the knowledge of the Secret of Charlotte Brontë, brought to us by Dr. Paul Heger's generous gift of these pathetic and beautiful Love-letters, the 'Problem of Charlotte Brontë,' as so many very clever but inattentive psychological critics have stated it, has lost all claim to serious attention.

The basis of the 'Problem' was the alleged 'dissonance' between Charlotte's personality and her genius—between her dreary, desolate, dull, well-tamed existence, uncoloured, untroubled by romance (as Mrs. Gaskell painted it), and the passionate atmosphere of her novels, where all events and personages are seen through the medium of one sentiment—tragical romantic love.

We now know that the dissonance did not exist; that from her twenty-sixth year downwards, Charlotte's life was, not only coloured, but governed by a tragical romantic love: that, in its first stage, threw her into a hopeless conflict against the force of things and broke her heart: but that, because the battle was fought in the force, and in the cause, of noble emotions, saved her soul alive; and called her genius forth to life: so that it rose as an immortal spirit from the grave of personal hopes.

Understanding this, we know that there is no 'Problem' of Charlotte Brontë: but that her personality and her genius and her life and her books were all those of a Romantic. But although there is no psychological Problem, a difficulty that concerns the historical criticism of Charlotte's life and her books does remain. And this difficulty has to be faced and conquered, not by speculations nor arguments, but by methods of enquiry.

When we study Charlotte Brontë's masterpiece *Villette* in comparison with what we now know about the romance in her own life, we recognise two facts: the first is that, *in this work especially*, she has painted with such power the emotions she has undergone that her words become feelings that lift and ennoble the reader's sensibility: and thus serve him—in the way that it belongs to Romantics to serve mankind.

But the second fact we discover is that,—again, *in this book particularly*,—historical personages and real events are used as the materials for an imaginary story, in a way that has produced critical confusion: and what is graver still—has caused false and injurious opinions to be formed about historical people. And the difficulty we have to face is, not what amount of blame belongs to Charlotte for misrepresenting historical facts, nor even need we ask ourselves what reason she had for thus misrepresenting them. Because the reason becomes plain when we take the trouble to realise that the motive the writer of this work of genius had in view was one that concerned her own personal liberation from haunting memories, rather than any motive concerning the impressions she might produce.

There can be no doubt that Charlotte's motive in *Villette*, judged as a method of personal salvation, was not only a permissible, but a noble one. It is the one that Pater attributed to Michael Angelo: '*the effort of a strong nature to attune itself to tranquillise vehement emotions by withdrawing them into the region of ideal sentiments*':—'*an effort to throw off the clutch of cruel and humiliating facts by translating them into the imaginative realm, where the artist, the author, the dreamer even, has things as he wills, because the hold of outward things*' (such a stern and merciless one in the case of Charlotte Brontë!) '*is thrown off at pleasure.*'

But, judged as a literary and historical method, was Charlotte

Brontë's manner of treating the real Director and Directress of the Pensionnat in the Rue d'Isabelle a justifiable or fair one? Can she be held without fault in this; that in Paul Emanuel and in Madame Beck she painted Monsieur and Madame Heger in a way that rendered them visible to every one who knew them; and then placed them in fictitious circumstances that altered the character of their actions and feelings, in such a way as to misrepresent their true behaviour? It seems to me that we must admit that the authoress of the *Professor* and of *Villette* adopted an unjust literary and historical method in so far as these real people are concerned: and that in the case of Madame Heger especially, passion and prejudice betrayed her: and rendered her guilty of a fault that must be recognised as a very grave one. But when this fault has been recognised and admitted, it seems to me a conscientious critic's duty does not compel him to scold this woman of genius for having the passions of her kind. A great Romantic is not an angel: and in this case the main facts about Charlotte are not her shortcomings as a celestial being, but her transcendent merits as an interpreter of the human heart. For my own part, I confess that after reading Charlotte's Love-letters, I am in no mood to look for faults in her, nor even to lend much attention to some faults that, without looking for them, one is bound to recognise. For what a thankless and unseemly, as well as what an unprofitable, sort of criticism is that represented in ancient days by the youngest amongst Job's Friends, who had such a delightfully expressive name, Elihu, the son of Barachel the Buzite, of the kindred of Ram! Elihu's criticism of Job (the man of genius, plunged into dire misfortune, not by any fault or folly of his own, but by the will of the Higher Powers, who desired to prove his virtue and to call forth his genius), is exactly the same method of criticising men and women of genius in the same case as Job, practised by Elihu's intellectual descendents, Buzites of the kindred of Ram, in all countries and in every age, down to England in the twentieth century. The fundamental doctrine of this critical method was, and is, that '*great men are not always wise,*' and that it is the vocation of smaller men to teach them wisdom, without 'respecting their persons or giving them flattering titles' (truly, as a matter of fact, by calling them names—knaves, hypocrites, sentimental cads, blackguards, etc.). In other words, the rule with these Buzites is that the main purpose of criticising great people is *to find fault with them*; to surprise them in their 'unwise' moments, to concentrate attention upon the faults they may, or may not, have committed in these moments; and to build upon these occasional real, or imaginary, faults, psychological and pathological theories about the madness, wickedness, or folly of people capable of them. And to conclude that there is 'very much to reprobate and a great deal to laugh at' in these men and women of genius—and that the fact that they had genius, and that as witnesses to the 'instinct of immortality in mortal creatures' they have served and honoured mankind, and also have bequeathed to us treasures of ideal beauty, is a mere accident, and may be left unnoticed.

But let not *my* portion ever be with these fault-finders, who '*darken counsel by words without knowledge*,' as the original Elihu was told, 'out of the Whirlwind,' by the Supreme Critic; 'in whose stead' the son of Barachel had arrogated to himself the right to scold and scoff at Job; and to tell him that his misfortunes were all the result of his bad character and of his uncontrolled emotions. I refuse, then, to recognise as a question of vital importance Charlotte's forgetfulness of historical exactitude in *Villette*; and I do not myself understand how any one (except a Buzite) who has read these Letters given to us by Dr. Paul Heger, and especially the last one, that received no answer, can help feeling that the suffering the writer of the Letters must have undergone, in the unbroken silent solitude that followed her unanswered appeal, must have made the hold upon her memory of 'outward things' so hard to bear, that to break that hold, to live in the realm of imagination free from it, *having things as she would*, justified almost any method of self-liberation.

Still the fact of the critical confusion of the personages in the novel with the historical Director and Directress of the Pensionnat in the Rue d'Isabelle does create difficulties in the way of forming right opinions. And to remove them, we have to follow the plan already recommended,—to make sure of our facts, before calling in the aid of psychological arguments. And in this case, to see the position clearly, we must disentangle from the imaginary story in *Villette* the real personages and events woven into the fabric of a parable where, as I have said, they appear amongst fictitious circumstances and produce consequently false impressions. In other words, we have to recover a clear knowledge of the true Monsieur Heger before we can determine where 'Paul Emanuel' resembles, and where he differs from, the Professor, *whom Charlotte loved: but who never showed any particle of love for Charlotte, such as Paul Emanuel bestowed on Lucy Snowe.* And then we have to re-establish in her true place, as Monsieur Heger's wife and the mother of his five children, the true Directress of the Pensionnat in the Rue d'Isabelle—who must be contrasted, rather than compared, with the crafty, jealous and pitiless Madame Beck of the novel, selfishly and cruelly interfering with the true course of an entirely legitimate and romantic attachment between her English teacher and her cousin, the Professor of literature. And the relative positions of these two Directresses clearly seen, we have to ask ourselves, Whether the real Madame Heger is proved to have had the base and detestable character of the hateful Madame Beck? and whether she really *was*, in any voluntary or even involuntary, way, the direct cause of poor Charlotte's anguish, suspense and final heart-break? And whether, given the positions and the different views of life and sense of duty of the different people whose destinies become entangled in this tragical romance, we can find fault with any person concerned in these events,—unless, indeed, we follow Greek methods, and drag in the Eumenides? Or, else, suppose it a parallel case with Job's: and decide that it was the will of the Higher Powers to prove Charlotte's virtue and to call forth her genius? But in so far as mere mortals are concerned, we have to see whether anything else could have happened, and whether poor Charlotte was not bound to break her heart?

So that the purpose of the Second Part of this study of the 'Secret of Charlotte Brontë' really lies outside of the 'Secret' itself, and becomes an effort to know 'as in themselves they really were,' and independently of their relationships with Charlotte, the Professor whom she loved (probably much more than he deserved), and the Directress of the Pensionnat in the Rue d'Isabelle—whom she certainly hated, without any reasonable cause for this hatred, although this hatred had a natural cause—that if only we will use psychology for the purpose of penetrating facts, and not for playing with such fictions as that *it was 'no serious grief to Charlotte that Monsieur Heger was married'* we may easily discover. After all, one must not ask for entire 'reasonableness' from Romantics, who see personages and events through the medium of one great Passion. And one must not demand from them absolute impartiality, when judging the impediment that divides them from the object of this passion.

We are not judges then in this case, but enquirers into the facts of the personality and true characters of the Director and Directress of the Bruxelles school and of their environment, as the influences that so largely created the Romantic atmosphere where Charlotte's genius lived and moved and had its being. And, by the special circumstances of my own life, I am able to assist in a way that is not (so I am tempted to believe) possible to any other living critic. The difficulty that stands in the way of most modern investigators is that long ago the historical people with their environment 'have become ghostly.' Long ago, for most readers of *Villette*, the once famous Pensionnat de Jeunes Filles in the Rue d'Isabelle, with its memory-haunted class-rooms, with its high-walled garden in the heart of a city whose voices reached one, as from a world far away, and 'down whose peaceful alleys it was pleasant to stray and hear the bells of St Jean Baptiste peal out with their sweet, soft, exalted sound,' have vanished out of life. *Yes—but out of my life they have not vanished!* For me—the historical Monsieur and Madame Heger exist quite independently of all associations with the imaginary personages Paul Emanuel and Madame Beck. For me—the old school, the class-rooms, the walled garden, with its ancient pear-trees that still 'faithfully renewed their perfumed snow in spring and honey-sweet pendants in autumn,' remain—as they were planted vivid images and visions in my memory half a century ago, when, as a schoolgirl, I knew nothing about Charlotte Brontë nor *Villette*: but when I sat, twenty years after Charlotte, in the class-rooms where she had waited for M. Heger, on the eve of her departure from Bruxelles, myself an attentive pupil of her Professor, and a witness, half terrified, and half exasperated, of his varying moods. And when, too, I saw, rather than heard, Madame Heger, moving noiselessly, where M. Heger's movements were always attended with shock and excitement; only to me, Madame Heger appeared always a friendly rather than an adverse presence—an abiding influence of serenity that reassured one, after sudden recurrent gusts of nerve-disturbing storms.

And I would point out that the value of my testimony about the personal impressions I derived, quite independently of any knowledge of Charlotte Brontë's residence in what was for me *my* school, and of her enthusiasm for *my* Professor, or her dislike of *my*schoolmistress, is enhanced both by the resemblances and by the differences of our several points of view. Thus—like Charlotte—I was an English pupil and a Protestant in this Belgian and Catholic school. Like her—my vocation was to be that of a woman of letters. And although, when she was brought under M. Heger's influence, she was a woman of genius, already well acquainted with good literature, and not without experience as a writer, whereas I was only an unformed girl, with very little reading and no culture: and merely by force of an inborn desire to follow a certain purpose in life that filled me with happiness, even in anticipation, justified in supposing that I had a literary vocation at all, and although no doubt I have not turned my advantages to account as Charlotte did, yet I myself owe to M. Heger, not only admirable rules for criticism and practice, that have always claimed and still claim my absolute belief, but also I owe to him, as she did, a full enjoyment of beautiful thoughts, beautifully expressed, and of treasures of the mind and of the imagination, that, lying outside of the recognised paths of English study, I might never have found, nor even have recognised as treasures, had I not been cured of insularity of taste by M. Heger.

So that upon this point I am able to say of M. Heger what Charlotte said: he was the only master in literature I ever had; and up to the present hour I esteem him, in this domain of literary composition, the only master whose rules I trust.

But if my judgment of M. Heger, as a Professor, coincides with Charlotte's, my judgment of him, outside of this capacity, does not show him to me at all as the model of the man from whom she painted Paul Emanuel. In other words, I never found nor saw in the real Monsieur Heger the lovableness under the outward harshness,—the depths of tenderness under the very apparent severity and irritability,—the concealed consideration for the feelings of others, under the outer indifference to the feelings of any one who ruffled his temper; nor yet did I ever discover meekness and modesty in him, under the dogmatic and imperious manner that swept aside all opposition. In fact, I never found out that M. Heger wore a mask. But, irritable, imperious, harsh, not *unkind*, but certainly the reverse of tender, and without any consideration for any one's feelings, or any respect for any one's opinions, thus, *just as he seemed to be, so in reality, in my opinion, M. Heger actually was.* And what one must remember is that Charlotte's point of view, from which she formed the opinion that M. Heger *was* tender-hearted, and modest and meek, was the point of view of a woman in love; and this standpoint is not one that ensures impartiality.

My own point of view, between 1859 and 1861, was that of an English schoolgirl, under sixteen, of a Belgian schoolmaster, over fifty, who in his capacity of a literary Professor, was almost a deity to her; but who, outside of this capacity, was not a lovable, but a formidable man: a 'Terror,' in the sense children and nursery-maids give the term; that is to say, some one who is sure to appear upon the scene when one is least prepared to face him, and who is constantly finding fault with one. Now a 'Terror,' in this popular sense of the term, although he is not a lovable, is not necessarily a hateful personage. There may belong to him an interest of excitement, and even a secret admiration for his cleverness in fulfilling his role of taking one unawares and finding something in one to quarrel about. And most certainly this interest of excitement, and even of a sense of amusement, entered into my sentiment for M. Heger, whom I recognised as a double-being, an admirable literary Professor, but an alarming and irritating personality. But although I never hated him, I yet had some special grievances against this 'Terror,' not only because he had a trick of surprising me in weak moments, and of finding out my worst sides, but also because he was really, in my own particular case, unjust; and full of prejudice and impatience against my nationality, and personal idiosyncrasies that were not faults; and that I couldn't help. Thus he stirred up in me rebellious protests, that could not be uttered; because how was an English schoolgirl of fifteen to protest against the injustice of a Belgian 'Master,' in his own country, and his own school: who was a man past fifty, too; and what was more, in his capacity of literary Professor, if not quite a deity, at least, in my own opinion, the keeper of the keys of palaces where dwelt the Immortals?

And that my opinion of M. Heger's personality, as that of a 'Terror' (in the childish and popular sense) did really show me the man apart from the Professor very much as he really was, is confirmed by the first impression he made upon Charlotte herself before the glamour of romantic love had interfered with her critical perspicacity. Here is the original description of M. Heger, in the early days of her residence in Bruxelles:

'There is one individual of whom I have not yet spoken,' she wrote to Ellen Nussey, 'M. Heger, the husband of Madame. He is Professor of rhetoric: a man of power as to mind, but very choleric and irritable in temperament, a little black being, with a face that varies in expression. Sometimes he borrows the lineaments of a tom-cat: sometimes those of a delirious hyena: occasionally, but very seldom, he discards these perilous attractions and assumes an air not above one hundred degrees removed from mild and gentleman-like. He is very angry with me just now, because I have written a translation which he stigmatises as *peu correct.* He did not tell me so, but wrote the word on the margin of my book and asked me, in very stern *phrase*, how it happened that my compositions were always better than my translations, adding that the thing seemed to him inexplicable. The fact is that three weeks ago in a high-flown humour he forbade me to use either dictionary or grammar when translating the most difficult English composition into French. This makes the task rather arduous, and compels me every now and then to introduce an English word, which nearly plucks the eyes out of his head when he sees it. Emily and he don't draw well together at all.'

I am quoting this view of M. Heger's personality, taken by Charlotte Brontë before she became a partial witness, because, by and by, when I am giving my own reminiscences, it will be found that in 1842 M. Heger was very much the same Professor whom I knew in 1861.

And Madame Heger? Here too my impressions are obtained from a point of view unquestionably more impartial than Charlotte Brontë's. And it will be found that, when the alteration of clear power of vision that personal prejudices make has been realised, my opposite judgment of the Directress of the Pensionnat to the judgment of the authoress of *Villette*, is not the result of any difference in the *facts* of Madame Heger's characteristics and behaviour, but in the difference between the standpoints from which we severally judge them.

Charlotte's standpoint was the one of the devotee, of the great spirit who is neither a god nor a mortal, but the 'Child of plenty and poverty, who is often houseless and homeless'—and who cannot well see 'as in herself she really is,' the Mistress of the house; who prudently, *not necessarily with cruelty*, closes the doors of her home against intruders—that standpoint also is not one conducive to impartial judgments.

My own point of view was that of a girl on the threshold of womanhood, who saw in Madame Heger an embodiment of two qualities especially, that, perhaps because I did not possess them and could never possess them (passionate as I was by nature and with strong personal likings and dislikings), inspired me with a sentiment of reverence and wonder, as for a remote perfection, that, though unattainable, it did one good to know existed somewhere; just as it does one good, with feet planted on the earth, to see the stars. The qualities I saw in Madame Heger were serene sweetness, a kindness without preferences, covering her little world of pupils and teachers with a watchful care. *Tranquillité, Douceur, Bonté:* the French words express better than English ones the commingled qualities I felt existed in Madame Heger as she moved noiselessly (as Charlotte Brontë has described), whilst the more brilliant and gifted Professor's movements were always stormy.

When relating these reminiscences of Monsieur and Madame Heger and of the old school and garden, as I myself treasure them, and quite independently of their associations with Charlotte Brontë, I shall not be losing sight of the purpose that justifies this record (as an endeavour to disentangle fact from fiction) if, in so far as the facts that concern my own experiences are concerned, I ask now to be allowed to relate them in a different tone—that is to say, not any longer in the tone of a literary critic, nor as one supporting any thesis or argument, but simply as a story-teller 'who has been young and now is old.' And who, before the darkening day has turned to night, calls to remembrance scenes and personages long since vanished out of the world, but still alive for me, bathed in the light that shines upon the undimmed visions of my youth—although to almost every one else now alive these scenes have become 'as it were a tale that is told.'

CHAPTER II

MY FIRST INTRODUCTION TO CHARLOTTE BRONTË'S PROFESSOR

[1]

'Madame,—quelquefois, donner, c'est semer'—*Speech made to my Mother by M. Heger.*

In 1859 this memorable thing happened:—I was introduced by my mother to M. Heger as his future pupil. I was fourteen years of age: but I remember everything in connection with this event as though it had happened yesterday. We were staying at Ostend, where my mother had taken my brother and myself for a long summer holiday, because she believed we had been previously overworked at our former schools, from which she had removed us. She was convinced that we both of us stood in need of sea-air, exercise and healthy recreation, before we could take up our studies again, after the strain we had undergone. Upon this point my brother and I were entirely of one mind with our mother.

But after a holiday of three months, we had also begun to feel, with her, that this state of things could not go on for ever, and that—as she expressed it—'something had to be done with us.' What was done with us was the result of circumstances that I cannot but regard as fortunate, in my own case at any rate. They brought into my life, at a very impressionable age, influences and memories that have always been, and that are still, after more than half a century, extraordinarily serviceable and sweet to me.

The first of these fortunate circumstances was the renewal (due to an accidental meeting at Ostend) of my mother's friendship with a relative whom she had lost sight of for a great many years; who had married a Dutch lady and settled in Holland. The eldest daughter of these re-discovered cousins was an exceptionally charming girl of nineteen; and upon enquiry my mother found out that she had been educated at a school in Brussels, *situated in the Rue d'Isabelle, and kept by a certain Madame Heger.* How it came to pass that, only four years after the publication of *Villette*, and two years after Mrs. Gaskell's *Life of Charlotte Brontë*, it did not occur to my mother to identify this particular Brussels school with the one where the Director was the fiery and perilously attractive 'Professor Paul Emanuel' and where the Directress was painted as the crafty and treacherous 'Madame Beck,' I really cannot say; but, so it was. There can be no doubt that it was solely because the account rendered by her delightful young kinswoman of the school where she had spent three years was thoroughly satisfactory to my mother, and because the unaffected and accomplished girl herself was an excellent proof of the happy results of the education she had received, that my mother made up her mind that the best thing that could be 'done with me,' was to send me to Madame Heger's school. She had entered into correspondence with this lady, and the plan had developed into a further arrangement, that my brother was to be placed with a French tutor recommended by Madame Heger, and who was the Professor of History at her establishment. All these conditions were very nearly settled, when M. Heger came to visit my mother at Ostend; to talk matters over and to make final arrangements.

Of course from the point of view of my own humble interest I recognised that the visit of this Brussels Professor was an event of great importance. I was fully conscious of this, because my cousin had told me a great deal about M. Heger, explaining that *he* was the ruling spirit in the Pensionnat; that he was rather a terrible personage; and that *if he took a dislike to one,—well, he could be very disagreeable.* I had received so much advice upon this particular subject from my cousin that I had talked the matter over very seriously with my brother afterwards, and asked him what he thought I ought to do in order to avoid the misfortune of offending M. Heger. My brother's advice was sound:—'Don't let the man see you are afraid of him,' he said, 'and then, whatever you do, don't show off.'

Keeping these counsels in mind, after M. Heger's arrival, I sat upon the extreme edge of the rickety sofa that filled the darkest corner in the little salle-à-manger of our Ostend apartments over the Patissier's shop in the Rue de la Chapelle—I remember the very name of the Patissier; it was Dubois—watching and listening eagerly to the conversation of the Professor with my mother, who, strange to say, did not seem to be in the least afraid of him; nor to recognise that he was in any way different to ordinary mortals! And I must say, looking back to that September afternoon to-day, and realising our attitude of mind, my mother's and mine, towards this interesting personage to us, but interesting solely in his character of *my* future teacher, there does seem to me something amazing—so amazing as to be almost amusing—in our total unconsciousness of his already well-established real, or rather ideal claims as a personage immortalised in English literature, by an illustrious writer who, four years before my birth, had been his pupil; and whose romantic love for him, whilst it had broken her heart, had served as the inspiration of her genius; so that her literary masterpiece was precisely a book where the very school I was going to inhabit was painted, with extraordinary veracity, in so far as outward and local points of resemblance were concerned.

As for my own ignorance of all these circumstances there is nothing strange in that. Fifty-four years ago a schoolgirl of my age was not very likely to have read *Villette*. But what one may pause to inquire is whether if by any accident the book *had* come into my hands, and thus revealed to me my true position, should I have gone down on my bended knees to my mother, or to express the case more exactly, should I have flung my arms round her dear neck, and prayed, '*Don't send me to this school; I am afraid of Professor Paul Emanuel; I loathe Madame Beck; I shall never make friends with these horrid Lesbassecouriennes?*' Well, really, I don't think I should have done anything of the sort! At fourteen one adores an adventure. It seems to me probable that the excitement of going to the same school, and learning my lessons in the same class-rooms, and treading the paths of the same garden, and being instructed by the same teachers as a writer of genius, who had left these scenes haunted by romance, would have made me hold under all apprehensions of the Lesbassecouriennes as school-fellows, of the perfidious Directress with her stealthy methods of espionage, of the explosive, nerve-wrecking Professor, always breaking in upon one like a clap of thunder. Yes; but though held under, the apprehension would have troubled my inner soul a good deal all the same; and this would have been a pity. Because, in so far as the real Directress and real Belgian schoolgirls whom I was going to know in the Rue d'Isabelle went, these apprehensions would have been superfluous and misleading.

But now if there were no danger of my finding in the real Pensionnat any spiritual counterparts of either the fictitious Madame Beck, or of the perverted Lesbassecouriennes pupils, was it equally certain that, if I had read *Villette*, I should not have recognised and been justified in recognising in Monsieur Heger the original model and living image of that immortal figure in English fiction, '*the magnificent-minded, grand-hearted, dear, faulty little man*'—Professor Paul Emanuel?

We shall perhaps be able to decide this question better at the end of these reminiscences than here. But what must be realised is, that the very fact that lends some general interest to my mother's first impressions and my own about M. Heger is chiefly this: that it expresses observations made from a purely personal standpoint; out of sight of any literary views about 'Paul Emanuel,' or historical judgments upon his relations with Charlotte Brontë. The perfectly simple purpose we had in view was to see clearly what sort of a Professor M. Heger was going to prove, and whether I was going to do well as his pupil, and get on satisfactorily, amongst these foreign surroundings.

My mother formed a most favourable opinion of our visitor, and decided that I was fortunate in obtaining such a Professor. What had especially impressed her was a sentence delivered by M. Heger, with a masterly little gesture, that, as she herself said, entirely won her over to his opinions upon a question where elaborate arguments might have left her unconvinced. And I may observe here, that this belonged to M. Heger's methods, not so much of arguing, as of dispensing with arguments. His mind was made up upon most subjects, and as he had got into the habit of regarding the world as his class-room, and his fellow-creatures as pupils, he did not argue; he told people what they ought to think about things. And in order to make this method of settling questions not only convincing, but stimulating, to his most intelligent pupils, he held in reserve a store of these really luminous phrases, that he would use as little Lanterns, flashing them, now in this direction, now in that, but always with a special and appropriate direction given to the illuminative phrase, so that it lit up the point of view upon which he desired to fix attention. The particular sentence that conquered my mother's admiration and acquiescence in M. Heger's point of view was the one I have made the heading of this chapter. Here was how he contrived to introduce it. After discussing the plan of *my* studies, and the arrangements for my being taken to the English church by my brother every Sunday, and allowed to take walks with him upon half-holidays (to all of which of course I listened with passionate attention), they passed on to discuss the terms asked by the tutor whom the Hegers had recommended. My mother had been told by her Dutch cousin that they were exorbitant terms; and, as a matter of fact, I believe they were exactly twice the amount charged by the Hegers themselves: '*I am not a rich woman,*' my mother had said, apologetically, '*and I have put aside a fixed sum for my children's education; I doubt if I can give this.*' ... Then did the Professor see, and seize, his opportunity: '*Madame,*' he said, with a gesture, '*quelquefois, donner, c'est semer.*' My mother, dazzled with this prophetic utterance, remained speechless and vanquished. In the evening of the same day I heard her quote to the Dutch cousin, who did not approve of her consent to these charges, '*what that clever man, Professor Heger) said so well,*' as though it had been unanswerable. In the course of the next two years I often heard the same luminous phrase used, with equal appropriateness, to light up other propositions. (I have heard M. Heger use it in a sense where it became a different formula for expressing a fundamental doctrine of Rousseau, thus, '*Instruire, ce n'est pas donner, c'est semer,*' but I never heard the words without going back to the first impression, and to the vision it called up. I would see again the little *salle-à-manger* in the Rue de la Chapelle at Ostend, I would watch the masterly gesture of the Professor's hand when he delivered his triumphant sentence, that is not an argument, but is worth more; I would see the look of admiration and sudden conviction come into my dear mother's face; I would feel myself sitting upon the little rickety sofa in the dark corner, *and I would shudder with the foreknowledge of what was coming*, for, woebetide me that I should have to tell it, this first interview *did not leave with me the same impression of confidence in M. Heger as my future teacher and guardian that it did with my mother;* it left with me, on the contrary, the miserable conviction that the very worst thing that could have happened had happened; that M. Heger had taken a vehement dislike to me, and consequently that all hope of happiness for me in the Pensionnat in the Rue d'Isabelle was over and done with.

And the worst of it was, that it was all my own fault; or rather, to be just, it was my misfortune.

For I had had a really very bad time of it, sitting on that rickety little sofa. My mother, who had only too flattering an opinion of me in every way, had meant to say the kindest things about me to M. Heger, and I knew this perfectly. But unfortunately, although she spoke French with the greatest fluency and self-confidence (because as she was a very charming woman, and as Frenchmen are always polite in their criticism of the French of charming English women, she had been very often complimented upon her command of the language),—unfortunately, I say, her French was really English, literally translated; and every one who has experience of what false meanings can be conveyed by this sort of French will realise what I had suffered, because, though I only spoke French badly at this time, I understood the language better than my mother. And this is how I had heard myself described to my future Professor. My mother had *wished* to say that I was more fond of study and of reading than was good for the health of a girl of my age; but what she *actually* said was that I was fond of reading things that were not healthy or suitable (*convenable*) for a young girl. Again, she had*meant* to say that as I had worked too hard, she had let me run wild a little; and that consequently I might find it difficult to get into working habits again; but that as I had a capital head of my own, and plenty of courage, I should, no doubt, soon get into good ways again. But instead of all these flattering things (that might have been rather irritating too, only a Professor of experience knows how to forgive a parent's partiality), I had heard this fond mother of mine say that her daughter had recently contracted the habits of a little savage; and that it would require courageous discipline, as she was very headstrong, to bring her into the right way again. It will be understood that to sit and listen to all this about oneself was anguish. But, carefully watching M. Heger's face, I had a notion that he had found out there was some mistake. Still I was depressed and bewildered; and in dread of what I was going to say, when the time came, as I knew it must, when he would say something to me, and I should have a chance of answering for myself. And the misfortune was, that *when* the critical moment came, I wasn't expecting it; because, here, at least, what the author of *Villette* says of Professor Paul Emanuel was true of M. Heger—everything he did was sudden; and he always contrived to take one by surprise.

It was immediately after he had won his triumph over my

mother, and in the moment when I myself was under the spell of admiration for his talent, that he turned upon me, in a sort of flash, smiling down upon me (very red and startled to find him so near), and nodding his head with an irritating look of amusement as his penetrating eyes searched my doleful face. '*Aa-ah*,' he said, in a half-playful, but as it sounded to me, more mocking, than kindly tone, '*Aa-ah*' (another nod of the head), 'so this is the little Savage I have to discipline and vanquish, is it? And she is headstrong (*têtue*). Tell me, Mees, am I to be too indulgent? or too severe? (*Dois-je être trop indulgent? ou trop sévère?*') Now, if only I had made the natural reply, the one obviously expected from me—the one any girl in my position would have made, and which I myself should have made if I hadn't been addressed as 'a little savage,' and if I hadn't been smarting under the sense that he must have the worst possible opinion of me, and that I ought to vindicate my honour in some way,—if only, in short, I had remembered my brother's wholesome advice, '*Don't show off*,' that is to say, if only I had said, amiably and nicely, with a timid little smile, '*Trop indulgent, s'il vous plait, Monsieur*,' THEN all would have been well with me; M. Heger would have continued to smile; we should have exchanged amiable glances and parted the best of friends.... But of what use are these speculations? What I *did* reply to his question of whether he was to be too indulgent or too severe was—'*Ni l'un ni l'autre, Monsieur; soyez juste, celà suffit*' ... and I listened to the broadness of my own British accent, whilst I said it, in despairing wonder! M. Heger's smiles vanished; there came what I took to be a 'look of undying hatred' into his face—it was not perhaps so bad as all that, but ... well, I certainly hadn't conquered his favour. He said something disagreeable about Les Anglaises being over wise, too philosophical for him, which my mother thought was a compliment to my cleverness. But I knew what I had done, and that it could never be undone, henceforth ...

Well, but the case really was not quite so desperate perhaps?

THE SECRET OF
CHARLOTTE BRONTË

[1]This chapter is reproduced from the *Cornhill* by the kind permission of Messrs. Smith, Elder and Co.

CHAPTER III

MONSIEUR AND MADAME HEGER AS I SAW THEM; AND BELGIAN SCHOOLGIRLS AS I KNEW THEM

Let me give here my mother's, and my own, account of the impressions made upon us by M. Heger's personal appearance at this time.

'He is very like one of those selected Roman Catholic Priests,' my mother told her Dutch relatives, 'who go into society and look after the eldest sons of Catholic noblemen. He has too good a nose for a Belgian and, I should say, he has Italian blood in him.'

My own report, to my brother, who made anxious inquiries of me, was less flattering perhaps, but it was not intended to be disrespectful. I always see M. Heger as I saw him then: as too interesting to be alarming; but too alarming to be lovable.

'He is rather like Punch,' I said, 'but better looking of course; and not so good-tempered.'

Let me justify these two descriptions by showing that both of them were based upon an accurate observation of the man himself.

M. Heger, as I remember him, was no longer what Charlotte called him, angrily, in her letter to Ellen Nussey, a *little Black Being*, and, affectionately, under the disguise of Paul Emanuel, '*a spare, alert man, showing the velvet blackness of a close-shorn head, and the sallow ivory of his brow beneath.*' M. Heger in 1859 was still alert, but he was not spare, he was inclining towards stoutness. His hair was not velvet black, but grizzled, and he was bald on the crown of his head, in a way that might have been mistaken for a tonsure; and this no doubt added to the resemblance my mother saw in him to a Priest. He did not look in the least old, however. His brow, not sallow but bronzed, was unwrinkled; his eyes were still clear and penetrating (Charlotte said they were violet blue; and certainly she ought to have known. Still, *do violet eyes penetrate one's soul like points of steel?*) The Roman nose, that my mother thought too good a nose to be Belgian, and that reminded me of Punch (but a good-looking Punch) was a commanding feature. And the curved chin (also suggesting a good-looking Punch, to a young and irreverent observer), although it indicated humour, meant sarcasm, rather than a sense of fun. But Monsieur Heger had one really beautiful feature, that I remember often watching with extreme pleasure when he recited fine poetry or read noble prose:—his mouth, when uttering words that moved him, had a delightful smile, not in the least tender towards ordinary mortals, but almost tender in its homage to the excellence of writers of genius.

In brief, what M. Heger's face revealed when studied as the index of his natural qualities, was intellectual superiority, an imperious temper, a good deal of impatience against stupidity, and very little patience with his fellow-creatures generally; it revealed too a good deal of humour; and a very little kind-heartedness, to be weighed against any amount of irritability. It was a sort of face bound to interest one; but not, so it seems to me, to conquer affection. For with all these qualities of intellect, power, humour, and a little kind-heartedness, one quality was totally lacking: there was no love in M. Heger's face, nor in his character, as I recall it; and, oddly enough, looking back now to him as one of the personages in my own past to whom I owe most, and whose mind I most admire, I have to recognise that in my sentiment towards M. Heger to-day even, made up as it is half of admiration and half of amusement, there is not one particle of love.

I have said—in connection with my first impression, that 'undying hate' was the sentiment that M. Heger had conceived for me—that really 'it was not so bad as all that.' Still, what happened at this first interview, if it did not determine any deep-rooted antipathy to me, planted from this moment in M. Heger's breast, did indicate, to a certain extent, what the character of our future relationships was to be—*out of lesson-hours.* In these hours, our relationships of Professor and pupil were ideal. Seldom did an occasional misunderstanding trouble them. Certainly, in my own day, no other pupil entered with so much sympathetic admiration into the spirit of M. Heger's teaching as I did. He saw and felt this; and here I, too, was for him, and *as a pupil*, sympathetic. But in our personal relationships, there were certain things in me that were antipathetic to M. Heger, and that rubbed him so much the wrong way, that he was constantly (so it still seems to me) unjust to what were not faults, but idiosyncrasies, that belonged to my nationality and my character. First of all, there was my English accent: and here this singular remark has to be made: I never spoke such purely British French to any one as to M. Heger; and this was the result of my constant endeavour to be very careful to avoid the accent he disliked, when speaking to him. The second cause of offence in me was also due to my nationality, or rather to my upbringing. Like all English children of my generation, I had been brought up to esteem it undignified, and even a breach of good manners, to cry in public: and although I was tender-hearted and emotional, I was not in the least hysterical; and except under the stress of extreme distress, it cost me very little self-control not to weep, as my Belgian schoolfellows did, very often, at the smallest scolding; or even without a scolding, and simply because they were bored—'*ennuyée.*' I remember now my surprise, at first hearing the reply to my question to a sobbing schoolfellow: '*Pourquoi pleures-tu?* '*Parce que je m'ennuie.*' 'Why?' '*Mais je te le dis parce que je m'ennuie.*' Well, but M. Heger liked his pupils to cry, when he said disagreeable things: or, in any case, he became gentle, and melted, when they wept, and was amiable at once. But when one did not weep, but appeared either unmoved, or indignant, he became more and more disagreeable: and, at length, exasperated. A third idiosyncrasy in me that he disliked was not national, but personal. It was due to a sort of incipient Rousseau-ism,—that must have been inborn, because I was never taught it, even in England. And yet there it was, implanted in me as a sentiment, long before I recognised it as an opinion or conviction, that I could express in words! This natural sentiment, or principle, was the belief that '*I was born free: that my soul was my own: and that there was no virtue, wisdom, nor happiness possible for me outside of the laws of my own constitution.*' Unformulated, but inherent in me, this fundamental belief in myself as a law to myself, no doubt betrayed itself in a sort of independence of mind and manner very aggravating to my elders and betters, and to those put in authority over me. And especially aggravating to an authoritative Professor, who was, in all domains, opposed to individualism, and the doctrine of personal rights and liberty. Thus in literature M. Heger was a classic; in religion he was a dogmatic Catholic; in politics he was an anti-democrat, a lover of vigorous kings; and by constitution he was a king in his own right: a masterful man, not only a law to himself, but a lord, by virtue of his sense of superiority, to everyone else.

For these reasons, M. Heger and myself—on ideal terms as Professor and pupil—were on bad terms outside of lesson-hours. We could not quite dislike each other; but our relationships were stormy. There were, however, intervals of calm.

I have said that with a good deal of admiration, gratitude, and some amusement, there is no *love* for M. Heger intermingled with my remembrances of him.

There is, on the contrary, a good deal of love in the sentiment I retain for Madame Heger,—although, as a matter of fact, in the days when I was her pupil I never remember any strong or warm feeling of personal affection for her; nor have I any distinct personal obligation to her, as to one who, like M. Heger, rendered me direct services by her instructions or counsels. Nor yet again had Madame Heger any strong personal liking for me; nor did she show me any special kindness. But her kindness was of an all-embracing character. And so was her liking for, or rather love of, all the inhabitants of the little world she governed: a world that extended beyond the boundaries of the actual walls of the Pensionnat, in any stated year; a world, made up of all the girls who, before that year, and afterwards, through several generations, had been and ever would be, her 'dear pupils'; '*mes chères élèves*';—terms that, uttered by her, were no mere formula, but expressed a true sentiment, and a serious and, so it seems to me, a beautiful and sweet idealism. This idealism in Madame Heger, this constant love and care and watchfulness for the community of girls, who, passing out of her hands, were to go out into the world by and by, to fulfil there what Madame Heger saw to be the kind and sweet and tranquil, and sometimes self-sacrificing and sorrowful, mission of womanhood, enveloped the ideal school-mistress with a sort of unfailing benevolence, that became a pervading influence in the Pensionnat, singling out no particular pupils, and withdrawn from none of them.

Here, it seems to me, and not at all in the reasons imagined by Charlotte in the case of Madame Beck, we have the secret of Madame Heger's system of government. I really am not, at this distance of time, able to say positively whether there was, or was not, a surveillance that might be called a system of *espionage* carried on, keeping the head-mistress informed of the conversation and behaviour of this large number of girls, amongst whom one or two black sheep might have sufficed to contaminate the flock. I was not a faultless, nor a model girl by any means: but I was a simple sort of young creature with nothing of the black sheep in me; and I never remember in my own case having my desk explored, nor my pockets turned inside out. But if even this had been done, it would not have gravely affected me; because neither in my pockets nor in my desk, would anything have been found of a mysterious or interesting character. But I should think it very probable that, in this very large school, a watchful surveillance *was* kept up; and that if any of these schoolgirls, most of them under sixteen, had attempted, after their return from the monthly holiday, to bring back to school illegal stores of sweets, or a naughty story book, and had concealed such things in their school desks, well, I admit, I think it possible, that the sweets or naughty book *might* have been missing from the desk next day. And also that, in the course of the afternoon, a not entirely welcome invitation would have been received by the imprudent smuggler of forbidden goods to pay Madame Heger a visit in the Salon? These things took place occasionally I know: and naturally, amongst the girls public sympathy was with the smuggler. But I am not sure, if one takes the point of view of a Directress, if a large girls' school could be carried on successfully, were it made a point of honour that there should be no surveillance, and that pupils might use their lockers as cupboards for sweets, or as hiding-places for light literature.

But, apart from the fact that Madame Heger was, no doubt, both watchful and uncompromising in her surveillance, based upon a firm resolution that nothing 'inconvenient' must be smuggled in, or hidden out of sight, as a source of mischief in the school, there was in her no resemblance to the odious Madame Beck; that is to say, no *moral* resemblance. In physical appearance, the author of *Villette*did use Madame Heger evidently as the model for the picture of an entirely different moral person. '*Her complexion was fresh and sanguine, her eye blue and serene. Her face offered contrasts—its features were by no means such as are usually seen in conjunction with a complexion of such blended freshness and repose; their outline was stern; her forehead was high, but narrow; it expressed capacity and some benevolence, but no expanse.... I know not what of harmony pervaded her whole person.*'[1]

Taking this portrait from *Villette*, as it is given of Madame Beck, and comparing it with my own recollections, and also with the photograph I am fortunate enough to possess of Madame Heger at the age of sixty, it seems to me that this *is* a very accurate physical description of the real Directress of the school in the Rue d'Isabelle; who morally was as unlike the fictitious Madame Beck as truth is unlike falsehood. About the physical resemblance, I may say that, if I had trusted to my own impressions, I should have rejected the assertion that the 'outline of her features was stern.' I never remember associating sternness with Madame Heger; though her supreme quality of serenity imposed a sort of respect that had a little touch of fear in it. Upon re-examining the photograph attentively, however, I find that it is true that the outline of the features *is* stern; but I do not think that this impression was conveyed by the younger face, remembered with softened colouring; and lit up, as a characteristic expression, by a normal expression of serenity and of kindliness. '*I know not what of harmony pervaded her whole person*': that sentence of Charlotte's (used by her of the unspeakable Madame Beck) exactly expresses the impression I still retain of the very estimable and, by myself, affectionately remembered, Madame Heger.

MADAME HEGER AT SIXTY
(She was thirty years younger when Charlotte knew her)
From a portrait given to the author by Madame Heger's daughter
(Author's *Copyright*)

In the same way, as I have said, the apprehensions as to my future companions in this foreign school, that would infallibly have been awakened in me if I had read, before meeting them, the account given by the author of *Villette* of Belgian schoolgirls, as differing, not only in nationality, but in human nature, from English schoolgirls, would have been groundless. When I call up around me to-day the recollections of my Bruxelles schoolfellows, amongst whom I was the only English girl and the only Protestant, there does not come back to me any painful remembrance that I ever felt myself an alien amongst them. On the contrary, I remember privileges granted me as 'la petite Anglaise,' who was further away than others from home, and must be treated with special kindness. I see around me in this large company of girls, no 'perverted' nor precociously formed young women, *whose 'eyes are full of an insolent light, and their brows hard and unblushing as marble.'* In brief, I see no '*swinish multitude*'—such as insular prejudice, and a disturbed imagination, showed Charlotte; but I see very much the same mixed crowd of youthful faces, fair and dark, pretty and plain, smiling and serious, stupid and intelligent, coarse and fine, sympathetic and unlikeable, that one would get in such a large collection of English schoolgirls; but in all this crowd of my Belgian schoolfellows just what my memory does *not* show me anywhere, are the '*eyes full of an insolent light, and the brow hard and unblushing as marble,*'[2]—that are not characteristics of the schoolgirl in any nation or country I have ever known; and I have been a traveller in my time, and enjoyed opportunities of observing different national peculiarities, that never fell in the way of Charlotte, who spent two years in Bruxelles; but lived the rest of her life in Yorkshire.

As for the hundred (or more perhaps than a hundred) schoolgirls that made up in my day the little world ruled by Madame Heger as the administrator of a system based on the authority of *Douceur, Bonté*, and *les Convenances* (in the sense of what was seemly, and opposed to violence and ugliness), amongst them were many girls whom I only knew by name and sight; many of whom I knew slightly better, and whom I rather liked than disliked; a few whom I disliked heartily (very few of these)—and a few whom I loved dearly (very few again)—but amongst these friends, chosen because their hearts were in tune with my own, the difference of nationality and creed did not stand in the way of mutual affection. In some cases, it is true, life, with its exacting claims of duties and occupations and cares, rushed in to divide me afterwards from these companions of my best years; when everything that I am glad, and not sorry, to have been, and to have done, in a long life, was prepared and made possible for me—but at least one of these friendships formed with a Belgian schoolgirl in those days, I may describe as a life-long friendship: because it remains an unaltered sentiment that lives in me to-day, unquenched by the fact that, only a few years ago—after half a century had passed since we met—my girl friend that had been then, a white-haired woman now, died; in the same year, as it strangely happened, that our old school (transformed into a boys' college during the last twenty years of its existence), that had stood in the Rue d'Isabelle until 1909, was swept away, with its beautiful old walled garden and time-honoured pear-trees, that to the end of their lives 'renewed their perfumed snowy blossom every spring.'

I am told a handsome building now replaces the long, plain straggling façade of the historic school—but I have no wish to see it.

[1]*Villette*, chapter viii.

[2]See *Villette*, chapter viii.

THE SECRET OF
CHARLOTTE BRONTË

CHAPTER IV

MY SECOND INTERVIEW WITH M. HEGER. THE WASHING OF 'PEPPER.' THE LESSON IN ARITHMETIC

I had been an inmate of the school in the Rue d'Isabelle a fortnight. In this interval I had lived through a great deal. Thanks to attentive self-doctoring and a strict *régime*, where no luxuries in the way of private crying were allowed, I had pulled myself through the first acute stage of the sort of sickness that attacks every 'new' girl, as the result of being plunged into the cold atmosphere of a strange, and especially of a foreign, school. Now I was out of danger of the peril that had threatened me during about a week, the possible disaster of some sudden access of violent weeping over my sense of desolation, in the sight of these foreign teachers and pupils, that would have seemed to me profoundly humiliating, on patriotic, as well as upon private grounds. For, as the one English girl in this Belgian school, was not the honour of my country, or, at any rate, of the girls of my country, at stake? And then I realised, also, that politeness to the foreigner, as well as duty to myself and my country, forbade any exhibition of vehement home-sickness. Thus, might not these Belgian teachers and girls reasonably take offence, and say, 'Why do you come to school in our country if you don't like it? We didn't ask you to come here. Why don't you go home?'

By these methods, then, of what it pleased me to regard as a sort of philosophy of my own, I had lived through the worst, and if I was not entirely cured of occasional inward sinkings of the heart and the feeling of desolation, I felt I had mastered the temptation to make any public display of them. And having reached this point by my own effort, now help came to me in the shape of a friendly tribute and encouragement from a girl who was a sort of philosopher, also by a rule of her own, which she kindly explained to me, and which I entirely approved of. This girl was fair and small, and had broad brows and clear green eyes under them. Her name was Marie Hazard. She had not spoken to me before, but on several occasions had shown me little kindnesses, and given me nice smiles and nods of greeting. Finally she came up to me in the garden and took my arm:—

'Do you know why I have a friendship for you?' she asked.

'No,' I answered. 'But have you *really*? I *am* so glad.'

'Yes,' she proceeded to explain; 'I like you, because you are reasonable, and don't sit down and cry, as, of course, you *could* if you liked. I have as much heart as another; but it irritates me, and does not touch me one bit, to see some of the pupils here, the big ones too, crying and crying, and *why? because they have come back to school, and would rather be at home!* Evidently that is the case with all of us. And evidently, what is more, it's going to be the case for ten months. But for some insignificant holidays at the New Year, from now until August, thus it will be with us. We shall be all of us in this school, and we would all of us prefer to be in our homes. But why cry, then? or if one begins to cry, why leave off? Is one, then, to cry for ten months? And what eyes will one have at the end? And what good is it?'

I laughed, not only because she seemed to me to put it humorously, but because I was full of happiness that I had found a friend.

'Yes,' she said, 'you laugh, and that is well, too. It's the thing to do. Now, if *you* cried there might be an excuse; you are farther away from your people than we are. But you ask yourself, What is the good? And you say to yourself, No, I won't discourage the others. And that is English. And that is why I like the English; they are at least reasonable.'

This was balm to me. The sense of desolation had vanished.

Here was the proof that I had been a good witness, and served to uphold the good name of England, and also that I had conquered a friend.

I think it was the same afternoon, because there were Catechism classes, from which, as a Protestant, I was exempted, that I was sent out into the garden, for the first time, at an hour when no other pupils were there. Later on this privilege was very often accorded me, for the same reason; so that, in my own day at any rate, no one else in the school had the opportunity I had given me, and that I used, of taking possession of the enchanted place and making it my very own. And this was so because there was no knowledge in my mind at the time that Some One had been beforehand with me here; and that although for my inner self it became (and must always be for me exclusively) my own beautiful, well-enclosed, flower-scented, turf-carpeted, Eden where the spirit of my youth had its home before any worldly influences, or any knowledge of evil, had come between it and the poetry of its aspirations and its dreams, yet for every one *but* myself, it is Charlotte Brontë's Garden of Imagination, where *she* used to '*stray down the pleasant alleys and hear the bells of St. Jean Baptiste peal out with their sweet, soft, exalted sound.*[1]

And although no angel with a flaming sword—no, nor yet any Belgian architects and masons, who have broken down the walls and uprooted the old trees, and made the old historical garden in the Rue d'Isabelle a place of stones—can drive me out of *my* garden of memories where still (and more often than before as the day darkens) I walk 'in the cool of the evening' with the spirit of my youth; yet, for English readers, it is not I, but Charlotte Brontë who must describe, what I could never dare nor desire to paint after her, the famous *Allée défendue* that holds such a romantic place in her novel of Lucy Snowe, and that was also the scene of my second meeting with M. Heger.

'In the garden there *was a large berceau,*' wrote the author of *Villette*, '*above which spread the shade of an acacia; there was a smaller, more sequestered bower, nestled in the vines which ran along a high and grey wall and gathered their tendrils in a knot of beauty; and hung their clusters in loving profusion about the favoured spot, where jasmine and ivy met and married them ... this alley, which ran parallel with the very high wall on that side of the garden, was forbidden to be entered by the pupils; it was called indeed l'Allée défendue.'*

In my day there was no prohibition of the *Allée défendue*, although the name survived. It was only forbidden to play noisy or disturbing games there; as it was to be reserved for studious pupils, or for the mistresses who wished to read or converse there in quietude.

THE "ALLÉE DEFENDUE"

If I had a lesson to learn, it was to the *Allée défendue* that I took my book; and in this *allée* I had already discovered and appropriated a sheltered nook, at the furthest end of the *berceau*, where one was nearly hidden oneself in the vine's curtain, but had a delightful view of the garden. Before reaching this low bench, I had noticed, when entering the *berceau*, that a ladder stood in the centre; and that, out of view in so far as his head went, a man, in his shirt sleeves, was clipping and thinning the vines. I took it for granted he was a gardener, and paid no attention to him; but, in a quite happy frame of mind, sat down to learn some poetry by heart. My impression is that it was Lamartine's *Chûte des Feuilles*. Shutting my eyes, whilst repeating the verses out aloud (a trick I had), I opened them, *to see M. Heger.* He it was who had been thinning the vine; it was a favourite occupation of his (had I read *Villette* I should have known it).[2] Once again he took me by surprise, and I was full of anxiety as to what might come of it. Since I entered the school I had, indeed, caught distant views of him, hurrying through the class-rooms to or from his lessons in the First and Second divisions. But until my French had improved I was placed in the Third division, where M. Heger only taught occasionally, so that I had not yet received any lesson from him.

It was a relief to see that he looked amiable, and even friendly; if only I didn't lose my head and say the wrong thing again! One thing I kept steadily in view; nothing must induce me to forget my brother's advice this time; there must be no attempt at fine phrases, this time nothing that could possibly appear like showing off.... But all my anxieties upon this occasion were dispelled by the purpose of my Professor's disturbance of my studies. He invited me to assist him in washing a very stout but very affectionate white dog, to whom I was told I owed this service as he was a compatriot of mine, an English dog, with an English name: a very inappropriate one, for he was sweet-tempered and white, and the name was Pepper. For this operation of washing Pepper, I was invited upstairs into M. Heger's library, which was, in this beautifully clean and orderly house, a model of disorder; clouded as to air, and soaked as to scent, with the smoke of living and the accumulated ashes of dead cigars. But the shelves laden from floor to ceiling with books made a delightful spectacle.

Upon the occasion of this first visit to his library, M. Heger made me the present of a book that marked a new epoch in my life, because, before I was fifteen, it put before me in a vivid and amusing way the problem of personality, *Le Voyage autour de ma Chambre* of Xavier de Maistre, was my introduction to thoughts and speculations that led me to a later interest in Oriental philosophy, and especially in Buddhism. I must not forget another present in the form of one more of those luminous little sentences that, as I have said, he used as Lanterns, turning them to send light in different directions. I had confided to him, not my own methods of philosophy—I did not dare incur the risk—but my newly found friend's methods of helping herself to be 'reasonable.' M. Heger showed no enthusiasm, nor even approval: and I found out that he had a strong dislike to my elected friend. Personally he would have preferred and recommended *Religious* methods of prayer, and docile submission to spiritual direction, to any philosophy, especially in the case of women. But he quoted to me and wrote down for me, and exhorted me to learn by heart and repeat aloud (as I actually did), a definition of the philosophy of life of an Eighteenth-century Woman, as '*Une façon de tirer parti de sa raison pour son bonheur.*' I discovered this sentence a great many years afterwards in a book of the de Goncourts. But M. Heger first gave it to me in my girlhood.

Although it was, of course, as Professor of Literature that M. Heger excelled, he was in other domains—in every domain he entered—an original and an effective teacher. Let me give the history of a famous Lesson in Arithmetic by M. Heger that took place, I am not quite sure why, in the large central hall, or *Galerie* as it was called, that flanked the square, enclosing the court or playground of daily boarders, whilst the *Galerie* divided the court from the garden. For some special reason, all the classes attended this particular lesson; where the subject was the *Different effects upon value, of multiplication and division in the several cases of fractions and integers.* Madame Heger and the Mesdemoiselles Heger, and all the governesses were there. I had been promoted into the first class (passing the second class over altogether) before this, so that I was a regular pupil of M. Heger's in literature, and certainly in this class, a favourite. But I was a complete dunce at arithmetic, and it was a settled conviction in my mind that my stupidity was written against me in the book of destiny; and I admit that, as it did not seem of any use for me to try to do anything in this field, I had given up trying, and when arithmetic lessons were being given I employed my thoughts elsewhere. But a lesson from M. Heger was another thing; even a lesson in arithmetic by him might be worth while. So that I really did, with all the power of brain that was in me, try to apply myself to the understanding of his lesson. But it was of no use; after about five minutes, the usual arithmetic brain-symptoms began; words ceased to mean anything at all intelligible. It was really a sort of madness; and therefore in self-defence I left the thing alone and looked out of the window, whilst the lesson lasted. It never entered my head that *I* was in any danger of being questioned: no one ever took any notice of me at the arithmetic lessons. It was recognised that, here, I was no good; and as I was good elsewhere, they left me alone. Yes, but M. Heger wasn't going to leave me alone. Evidently he had taken a great deal of trouble, and wanted the lesson to be a success. And it had not succeeded. He was dissatisfied with all the answers he received. He ran about on the *estrade*getting angrier and angrier. And then at last, to my horror, he called upon *me*; and what cut me to the soul, I saw that there was a look of confidence in his face, as if to say 'Here is some one who will have understood!'

... Well of course the thing was hopeless. I had a sort of mad notion that a miracle might happen, and that Providence might interfere, and that if by accident I repeated some words I had heard him say there might be some sense in them—but, as Matthew Arnold said, miracles don't happen. It was deplorable. I saw him turn to Madame Heger with a shrug of the shoulders: and that he must have said of the whole English race abominable things, and of this English girl in particular, may be taken for granted; because Madame Heger hardly ever spoke a word when he was angry. But now she said something soothing about the English nation, and in my praise. Well, my case being settled, M.

Heger began: and he did not leave off until the whole Galerie was a house of mourning. In the whole place, the only dry eyes were mine, and here I had to exercise no self-control; for although at first I had been sorry for him, now I was really so angry with him for attacking these harmless girls, and attributing to them abominable heartlessness, although the place rang with their sobs, that I don't think I should have minded a slight attack of apoplexy—only I shouldn't have liked him to have died.

It was really a bewildering and almost maddening thing, because on both sides it was so absurd. First of all, what had all these weeping girls done to deserve the reproaches the Professor heaped upon them? 'They said to themselves,' he told them: '"What does this old Papa-Heger matter? Let him sit up at night, let him get up early, let him spend all his days in thinking how he can serve *us*, make difficulties light, and dark things clear to *us*. *We* are not going to take any trouble on our side, not we! why should we? Indeed, it amuses us to see him *navré*—for us, it is a good farce."'

The wail rose up—'*Mais non, Monsieur, ce n'est pas vrai, cela ne nous amuse pas; nous sommes tristes, nous pleurons, voyez.*'

The Professor took no heed; he continued. 'They said to themselves "Ah! the old man, *le pauvre vieux*, takes an interest in us, he loves us; it pleases him to think when he is dead, and has disappeared, these little pupils whom he has tried to render intelligent, and well instructed, and adorned with gifts of the mind, will think of his lessons, and wish they had been more attentive. Foolish old thing! not at all," they say, "as if *we* had any care for him or his lessons."'

The wail rose up—'*Ce n'est pas gentil ce que vous dites là, Monsieur: nous avons beaucoup de respect pour vous, nous aimons vos leçons; oui, nous travaillerons bien, vous allez voir, pardonnez-nous.*'

'Frankly, now, does that touch you?' I heard behind me. 'It is not reasonable! I find it even stupid (*je le trouve même bête*).' Marie Hazard, of course. I made a mistake when I said *my* eyes were the only dry ones. Here was my philosopher-friend, amongst the pupils in the Galerie, and her eyes were quite as dry as mine.

But the story of the Lesson in Arithmetic does not finish here; and nothing would be more ungrateful were I to hide the ending: by which I was the person to benefit most. To my alarm, in the recreation hour next day, M. Heger came up to me, still with a frowning brow and a strong look of dislike, and told me he wished to prove to himself whether I was negligent or incapable. Because if I was incapable, it was idle to waste time on me—so much the worse for my poor mother, who deceived herself! On the other hand, if I was negligent, it was high time I should correct myself. This was what had to be seen. I followed him up to his library, not joyously like the willing assistant in the washing of Pepper, but like a trembling criminal led to execution. I felt he was going again over 'fractions' and the 'integers.' I knew I shouldn't understand them; and that he wouldn't understand that I was 'incapable,' that when arithmetic began my brain was sure to go!

The funny and pleasant thing about M. Heger was that he was so fond of teaching, and so truly in his element when he began it, that his temper became sweet at once; and I loved his face when it got the look upon it that came in lesson-hours: so that, whereas we were hating each other when we crossed the threshold of the door, we liked each other very much when we sat down to the table; and I had an excited feeling that he was going to make me understand. *It took him rather less than a quarter of an hour.*

On the table before us he had a bag of macaroon biscuits, and half a Brioche cake. He presented me with a macaroon. There you have one whole macaroon (*intègre*): well, but let us be generous. Suppose I multiply my gift, by eight: now you have eight whole macaroons and *are eight times richer*, hein? But that's too many; *eight* whole macaroons! I divide them between you and me. As the result, you have half the eight. But now for our *half-Brioche*; we have one piece only: and we are *two people*, so we multiply the pieces. But *each is smaller*, the more pieces, the smaller slice of cake; here are eight pieces; they are really too small for anything, we will divide this collection of pieces into two parts. Now does not this division make you better off, hein? Then he folded his arms across his chest in a Napoleonic attitude, and nodding his head at me, asked, '*Que c'est difficile,—n'est-ce pas*?'

Of course in this, and indeed in all his personal and special methods, M. Heger followed Rousseau faithfully. But, then, where is the modern educationalist since 1762 who does *not* found himself upon Rousseau?

It was not, however, in rescuing one from the slough of despond, where natural defects would have left one without his aid, that M. Heger excelled—it was rather in calling out one's best faculties; in stimulating one's natural gifts; in lifting one above satisfaction with mediocrity; in fastening one's attention on models of perfection; in inspiring one with a sense of reverence and love for them, that M. Heger's peculiar talent lay.

I may attempt only to sum up a *few* maxims of his, that have constantly lived in my own mind: but I feel painfully my inability to convey the impression they produced when given by this incomparable Professor; whose power belonged to his personality; and was consequently a power that cannot be reproduced, nor continued by any disciple. The Teacher of genius is born and not made.

The first of these maxims was that, before entering upon the study of any noble or high order of thoughts, one had to follow the methods symbolised by the Eastern practice of leaving one's shoes outside of the Mosque doors. There were any number of ways of 'putting off the shoes' of vulgarity, suggested to one's choice by M. Heger: the reading of some beautiful passage in a favourite book; the repetition of a familiar verse: attention to some very beautiful object: the deliberate recollection of some heroic action, *etc.* With different temperaments different plans might be followed:—what was necessary was that one did not enter the sacred place without some *deliberate* renunciation of vulgarity and earthliness: by *some* mental act, or process, one must have 'put off one's shoes.' There is here a strange circumstance that I was too young to feel the true importance of at the time, but that I have often wondered over since then. There can be no doubt of M. Heger's rigid orthodoxy as a Catholic. Yet whilst the recitation of the Rosary inaugurated the daily lessons, M, Heger had a special invocation[3] of 'the Spirits of *Wisdom, Truth, Justice, and Equanimity,*' that was recited by some chosen pupil; who had to come out of her place in class and stand near him; and who was not allowed by him to gabble. And this was the invariable introduction to *his* lesson. I can't feel it was an orthodox proceeding: *There was not a Saint's name anywhere!* But I feel the infallible impression it produced upon me now. One effect, in the sense of 'putting off one's shoes,' that it had for myself was that the Professor of Literature appeared to me without any of the dislikable qualities of the everyday M. Heger.

Another maxim of M. Heger's was certainly borrowed from Voltaire: That one must give one's soul as many forms as possible. *Il faut donner à son âme toutes les formes possibles.* Again, that every sort of literature and literary style has its merits, *except the literature that is not literary and the style that is bad:* here again, one has, of course, Voltaire's well-known phrases: *J'admets tous les genres, hors le genre ennuyeux.*'

A third maxim was that one must never employ, nor tolerate the employment of, a literary image as *an argument*. The purpose of a literary image is to illuminate as a vision, and to interpret as a parable. An image that does not serve both these purposes is a fault in style.

A fourth maxim is that one must never neglect the warning one's ear gives one of a *fault* in style; and never trust one's ear exclusively about the merits of a literary style.

A fifth rule:—One must not fight with a difficult sentence; but take it for a walk with one; or sleep with the thought of it present in one's mind; and let the difficulty arrange itself whilst one looks on.

A sixth rule:—One must not read, before sitting down to write, a great stylist with a marked manner of his own; unless this manner happens to resemble one's own.

Now I shall be told that these rules and maxims, whether true or false, are 'known to nearly every one,' and are of assistance to no one; because people who can write do not obey rules: and people who can't write are not taught to do so by rules. If this were literally true then there would be no room in the world for a Professor of Literature. My own opinion is that there are very few good writers who do not obey rules; and that these rules are, if contracted in youth, of great use as a discipline that saves original writers from the defect of their quality of originality, in a proneness to mannerisms and whims.

In connection with the possible complaint that I am putting forward as M. Heger's maxims, sentences that were not originally invented nor uttered by him, my reply is that I do not affirm that he invented his own maxims, but simply that he chose them from an enormous store he had collected by study and fine taste and by a sound critical judgment, the result of an extensive acquaintanceship with the best that has been said and thought in the world by philosophers, poets, and literary artists and connoisseurs. In his character of a Professor of literature I find it hard to imagine that any gift of original thought, or personal power of expressing his own thoughts, could have placed M. Heger's pupils under the same obligations as did his knowledge of beautiful ideas, beautifully expressed, gathered from north, south, east and west, in classical, mediæval and modern times. To be given these precious and luminous thoughts in one's youth, when they have a special power to 'rouse, incite and gladden one,' is a supreme boon:—and in my own case my gratitude to M. Heger has never been in the least disturbed by the discovery that he was not the inventor of the maxims that have constantly been a light to my feet and a lantern to my path during the half-century that has elapsed since I received them from him in the historical Pensionnat, that stood for many years, after Monsieur Heger himself had vanished out of life, but that stands no longer in the Rue d'Isabelle.

[1]From Mlle. Louise Heger I have this note: '*Les cloches de St. Jacques et non pas St. Jean Baptiste, église qui se trouve à l'autre côté de la ville près du canal: quartier du Père Silas dans "Villette."*'

[2]*Villette*, chapter xii.

[3]Esprit de Sagesse, conduisez-nous:
Esprit de Vérité, enseignez-nous:
Esprit de Charité, vivifiez-nous:
Esprit de Prudence, préservez-nous:
Esprit de Force, défendez-nous:
Esprit de Justice, éclairez-nous:
Esprit Consolateur, apaisez-nous.

Here is the invocation, sent me by Mlle. Heger; who has, with extreme kindness, endeavoured to recover it for me.

CHAPTER V

THE STORY OF A CHAPEAU D'UNIFORME

In connection with the particular Belgian schoolgirls whom I knew, who still, in 1860, learnt their lessons in the class-rooms where Charlotte Brontë once taught, and who were still taught by M. Heger, and still surrounded with the benign and serene influences of Madame Heger, let me prove that these schoolgirls had not the characteristics of the *Lesbassecouriennes*; and that Charlotte Brontë displayed insular prejudice, as well as an imagination coloured by the distress of an unhappy passion, when she said of them, '*The Continental female is quite a different being to the insular female of the same age and class.*'[1]

Inasmuch as the story I have to tell is the story of a Bonnet, it will be recognised as one that is calculated to display the qualities and intimate and essential peculiarities of the 'Continental female' (under sixteen) in a light, and under the stress and strain of passions and interests, too serious to permit of any tampering with, or disguise of, nature. One has to realise, also, that the question is not merely of a bonnet, but of a Best Bonnet, a Sunday Bonnet. For, in the remote days of which I am now writing modern young people should realise even schoolgirls of ten or twelve wore bonnets on Sunday, and even upon week-days, when they went beyond the borders of their garden: a hat was thought indecorous on the head of any girl in her 'teens—a form of undress rather than of dress. To wear a hat was like wearing a pinafore—a confession that one had not forgotten the nursery. To save one's best Sunday Bonnet, in the garden, one might go about in a hat, and in the bosom of one's family wear a pinafore to save a new dress; but in the same way that one did not go into the drawing-room with a pinafore on, one did not, in those days, pay visits in a hat: and to go to church in one would have been thought irreverent. So that a Sunday Bonnet meant that childish ways were done with, and that one had attained the age of reason. Like a barrister's wig it imposed seriousness on the wearer, who had to live up to it. Madame Heger, when establishing the rules for the uniform that was worn by all the pupils of the school in the Rue d'Isabelle, paid great attention to the Sunday Bonnet. Following the sense she lent to the law of her system of government, the love of dress was not to be allowed amongst her pupils to become an encouragement to vanity and rivalship, and hence one uniform, for rich and poor alike, avoided any chance of vain, unkind, and envious feelings; but at the same time the love of dress was not to be discouraged altogether; because it was serviceable to taste, and the care for appearance, without which a young person remains deficient in femininity. Therefore although every boarder wore the same uniform, what this uniform was to be was made quite an important question: and the girls were invited to choose a committee to decide it, in consultation with their head-mistress. And to this consultation Madame Heger brought a large spirit of indulgence, especially where the Sunday Bonnet was concerned. The Sunday Dress had to be black silk—about the *façon* there might be discussion, but not about the colour or material. On the other hand, about the Bonnet, everything was left an open question. It might be fashionable: it might be becoming: and even serviceableness was not made a too stringent obligation. Indeed in the first year of my school career the Sunday Bonnet selected for the summer months was the reverse of serviceable. It was white chip; it was decorated with pink rosebuds, where blonde and tulle mingled with the rosebuds; it had broad white ribands edged with black velvet—in short, a very charming Bonnet: but sown with perils. Everything about it could get easily soiled; and nothing about it would stand exposure to rain.

Madame Heger, recognising these material inconveniences, had nevertheless seen that, on the educational side, there were compensating advantages—the cultivation of neatness and order. She had not then discouraged the white chip, rosebuds and the rest; at the same time, she had stated the case for a yellow straw, with a plaid-ribbon that would not easily soil.

'On the one hand,' she had said, 'you may, with merely simple precautions, carry your Bonnet through the summer to the big holidays, without anxiety. On the other hand, no doubt there will be anxiety: the white chip is extremely pretty, but do not forget that it will require almost incessant care. Never must this Bonnet be put on one side without a clean white handkerchief to cover it. Not only so, one storm, if you have no umbrella, will suffice; everything will need renewal. And I warn you, my children, that if this misfortune arrive, it is not I, but *you*, who will have to ask your good mammas for another Bonnet. *I* ask from your parents a *chapeau d'uniforme*, and one only, each term: no more. So now decide as you please.'

The decision had been for the white chip, arrive what may. My own point of view, whilst the subject was being discussed around me, was that nothing could interest me less. Fancy troubling one's head about a Bonnet! I did not say it, because I had no wish to make myself unpopular, but the interest in the affair appeared to me puerile. Happily these trifling matters had no importance for me; it did not matter to me at all what sort of *chapeau d'uniforme* they chose.

How wrong I was! It mattered to me more than to any one else in the whole school, because no one wore their *chapeau d'uniforme* so much, and no one took the poor thing out so frequently into storm and rain. All the other boarders attended early mass on Sunday mornings in a convent chapel, within five minutes' walk of the school. The other occasions when they wore the fragile white chip *chapeau* were safe occasions, when, if it rained, they took shelter in their own homes on the monthly holidays, or were sent back to school in a *fiacre*. My case was different. Every Sunday morning, in accordance with the arrangement made by my mother, my brother called at the Rue d'Isabelle to take me to the English Church, which in those days was a sort of hall, known as the '*Temple Anglican*,' situated in a passage near the Bruxelles Museum. The service was generally over by noon; but it was too late for me to return to school in time for the déjeuner at mid-day, and this authorised the custom of my taking lunch with my brother and enjoying a short walk afterwards; so that I was taken back by him to the Rue d'Isabelle before four o'clock. Now it will be easily understood that this agreeable arrangement had temptations: and that *sometimes*, on *very* fine days, there would occur forgetfulness of the 'Temple Anglican' altogether; and the whole of these four or five hours would be spent in our favourite haunt, the Bois de la Cambre, where we would picnic, on cakes and fruit, when there was pocket-money enough, or on two halfpenny 'pistolets,' when, as often happened, ten centimes, that ought to have gone into the plate at the Temple, was all we had. And whether the lunch was of cakes, or of dry bread, it did not alter the fact that we talked of home incessantly; and were supremely happy. Yes; but no doubt our conduct was reprehensible, and did not deserve the favour of Heaven. And my recollection is that almost invariably these picnics in the Bois de la Cambre, to which an exceptionally fine day had tempted us, ended in a downpour of rain. And how it rains at Brussels, when it does rain! So now, think of the state of the white chip Bonnet, and of the bunch of rosebuds, interwoven with blonde, and of the white silk ribbon edged with black velvet, that I took back with me to the Rue d'Isabelle.

And it is here where the beautiful nature of Belgian schoolgirls, or of these particular Belgian schoolgirls who were my companions and contemporaries, stands revealed. For upon one particular Sunday, having hastily and silently fled to the dormitory upon my return, and being discovered there, in dismayed contemplation of the lamentable saturated mixture of mashed up tinted pulp and wires, that had once been rosebuds and blonde, my depths of despondency moved these sympathetic young hearts to compassion. As it was Sunday afternoon, one was allowed to loiter over getting ready for dinner; a circle of consolers gathered round me, and from it, forth stepped two rival aspirants to the honour of sacrificing themselves on the altar of friendship. The first said: 'Now nothing is more simple: we shall wrap up this unhappy rag in my handkerchief as you see;—*You shall have my chapeau d'uniforme*, and I shall tell Maman everything—she interests herself in you; for when she was young, she was at school in England. She will send me another*chapeau d'uniforme*, and all is said.'

The other girl, whose name was Henriette—I forget her surname—said, 'My plan is easier: for here is an accident,—as though it were done on purpose. Now what do you say: I have two *chapeaux d'uniforme*, if you please! The first my mother sent me as a model to show Madame Heger, and from this model she chose it. But now Madame had ordered mine with the others: and when I told my mother, she said, 'Say nothing: an accident may happen, the Bonnet will not support rain, you will have this one at hand if a misfortune arrive. Well, and here is the misfortune: there's no difficulty at all.'

Both of these girls had their homes in Brussels, and both of them I knew had everything their own way with two fondly indulgent mammas. I had no scruple in accepting their generous sacrifice, and I hugged them both, and was really (I who despised tears) on the verge of crying. Between the two, I hardly knew which offer to take, but it seemed to me that as Henriette had two Bonnets, it was most reasonable to take hers. And we all went down to dinner happily. And the 'Unhappy rag' '*cette malheureuse loque*,' was buried in the *hangar*, the wood-house at the bottom of the garden.

But under cloudless skies one is prone to forget the lessons of misfortune. It took some time—but the Sunday came when, once again, it seemed 'almost wrong' to waste summer hours in the Temple Anglican, when one felt so good under the beautiful trees in the Bois de la Cambre. And then there was pocket-money in hand, and a lunch of cakes, and not halfpenny pistolets, could be obtained.

'I suppose you don't think it will rain?' I suggested.

'Rain!' My brother said with scorn. 'Look at that sky! How could it rain?'

It managed to do it. True, it was only a brief shower: but the water came down in sheets. In despair I took off the *chapeau d'uniforme*, and my brother, who wore an Inverness cape, sheltered it under the flap. I stood to hold the cape at a right angle, so that the precious object might not be crushed, and we were watching it under this sheltering wing, and my brother was assuring me it was all right when,—as I stood there bareheaded and rain-beaten, beneath a tree by the side of the broad path near the entrance to the wood—a short, stoutish man, buttoned up to the chin in his greatcoat, and holding his umbrella tightly, walked by us at a great pace, without (so at least it seemed) looking at us at all. And that man was M. Heger. We gasped, and looked at each other.

'He didn't see us,' said my brother cheerily. 'What a bit of luck!'

'You may be quite sure he did see us,' I answered. 'Well, I wonder what will happen now?'

With this new anxiety on our hands, even the precious *chapeau d'uniforme* became a secondary consideration. But the shower having passed, we examined it carefully. There was no disaster this time. The rosebuds were still rosebuds and the blonde still blonde. It is true that a splash had fallen on the white chip crown, but my brother was always ready with comfort.

THE GALERIE AND GARDEN IN WINTER

(The Allée Defendue is on the left. The old pear-tree, whose lower branches still blossomed in spring, is on the right)

'When it's dry,' he told me, 'you'll easily get that off with a bit of bread.'

This consoled me for the time being: but he was wrong as to the question of facts. Bread had no effect upon that blot. It remained an island, or, to speak more correctly, a coast-line, on the white chip, to the end of that *chapeau d'uniforme*'s existence. But one dusted the stain over with white powder before putting on one's Bonnet, and hoped no one noticed it? So far as I know, no one did. But let it not be supposed that I escaped moral punishment: I, who had once boasted in my pride that nothing was less indifferent to me than my Sunday Bonnet, wore this one uneasily to the end of the term, always conscious that the tell-tale stain was there, and might suggest questions as to its origin.

Nor did I escape scot-free from M. Heger's hands, although he did behave with a certain generosity, for he kept the secret. But he used his own method of punishment.

Happy in the confidence given me by my brother's assurance that I should easily get rid of the rain-blot, I went back to the Rue d'Isabelle, in some anxiety about M. Heger, but *nearly* persuaded that, after all, perhaps, with his umbrella to think of and grasp, and the hurry he was in, he *very likely* hadn't seen us. But when the pupil's door was opened in answer to my ring, and I was hoping to hurry through the corridor to the staircase leading to the dormitories, I found M. Heger waiting for me. He barred my path and looked down at me with his penetrating, mocking eyes,—that, although I do not like to contradict Charlotte, I still think had more green and steel, than violet-blue, colour in them.

'A-ah,' he said with his long-drawn sigh, 'you are attentive at my lessons, Mees; do you now listen with the same attention to the sermon of the Minister at your Temple?'

Here was my opportunity; of course I ought to have said, '*No, Monsieur, I don't listen to any one with so much attention as I do to you: no one interests me so much.*' When I had got upstairs and had taken off the *chapeau d'uniforme*, I realised that this was what any rational being would have said. But it was too late then—all I did say was, '*Je ne sais pas, Monsieur*' (a bad French accent too).

'A-ah,' he repeated, tightening his mouth, 'now I should like to see whether you profit by the instructions of your Minister: Thus I shall be glad if you will write me a *résumé* in French of the sermon you heard to-day at the Temple. It will be a good exercise for you in the French language. And also I shall enjoy the happiness of knowing this wise Minister's advice. It is understood, you will give me the *résumé* of this sermon to-morrow.'

'*Oui, Monsieur.*'

All through the evening recreation hours, and at night when I fought against sleepiness in my bed, I worked over the composition of that sermon. It is true that I did fall asleep in the middle of it myself; but that does not prove it was a dull sermon, for I took it up again in the morning with renewed zest. I gave up my whole recreation hour after *déjeuner* to writing it out. And I believed it to be as good a sermon as was ever preached. And there was no vanity in this belief: because it was not my own sermon, but one I had originally heard preached in my childhood in an old village church, and the arguments in favour of being good and simple had taken hold of my imagination, partly on account of the associations with the place where I heard it. Well, but now, can my readers deny that when I say M. Heger was a more irritating than lovable man, I have sound reasons for my statement? *After ordering me to write that sermon, and when I had stolen several hours from my sleep, and given up two recreations to obey him, he never asked for it!* And when I told him I had written the sermon and that it was ready for him, he merely looked down upon me with a strange twinkle in his eyes, and said, '*A-ah, c'est bien. Vous l'avez donc bien retenu, ce fameux sermon? tant mieux, tant mieux.*'

[1]*Villette*, chapter viii.

CHAPTER VI

MADAME HEGER'S SENTIMENT OF THE JUSTICE OF RESIGNATION TO INJUSTICE

At the end of these reminiscences I have now to relate the incident that stands out in my memory as, not only the most bitter experience I had ever, up to this date, undergone of personal injustice in my brief life of fifteen years, not only, what was of great moral importance to me, my first lesson in the philosophy of refusing to torment oneself in order to punish one's tormentors, but also the incident that revealed to me a secret sorrow hidden away under Madame Heger's serenity; and that convinces me, now, that the tragical romance of Charlotte Brontë was not to her, as it must have been to M. Heger, misunderstood, and regarded as an event of small importance; but that it 'entered into her life,' and was to her a very serious trouble.

One day in June, I am not able to remember now upon what especial occasion, nor in honour of what event, all the school was given an entire holiday: and, for its better enjoyment, the girls were invited by a former pupil in the Rue d'Isabelle, who had married and possessed a fine château and a large garden within walking distance of Bruxelles, to spend the whole day in her house and garden, where a mid-day collation was prepared for them. I remember very little about the day's enjoyments—the cruel impressions that followed the pleasant holiday have effaced from my memory almost everything that preceded them. I know, however, that all was sunshine and good humour: that my companions whom I had trusted as friends were as friendly to me as ever; and that with my two chosen companions, the philosopher Marie Hazard and the other still dearer friend, who was a philosopher in a different sense, as a profound Nature-worshipper,—where *I* was supposed to be a philosopher in a sense of my own as a worshipper of ideas—talked 'philosophy' wisely and well—in our own estimation, and ate red gooseberries. As we talked other girls discovered these gooseberry-bushes also, and came in flocks: so we three withdrew, and sat down under some shady tree, and were very happy and at peace. Near us, on a low cane chair, sat one of the under-mistresses, a Frenchwoman, whom I liked extremely, and who also liked me: her name was Mlle. Zélie—she was too young to have been one of the mistresses known to Charlotte Brontë twenty years before. She may have been twenty-six: or she may have been thirty.

As she sat there, doing embroidery, and watching all the time a swarm of girls picking gooseberries,—we three, who had left off picking them, were at rest upon the grass,—there came, suddenly, a servant in great haste sent from the Rue d'Isabelle by Madame Heger, with a letter: neither Monsieur nor Madame had arrived yet, they were to be there in time for the collation in the afternoon. The letter was an urgent order to Mlle. Zélie that the girls were not to *touch the fruit in the kitchen garden*—this stipulation had been made by the generous hostess, who had invited all this company to a feast of cakes and cream and good things of every description, but who wanted her gooseberries and currants for jam. Here of course was cause of great dismay: although the bushes had not been entirely stripped, yet certainly thirty or forty girls amongst the gooseberry-bushes alone had made their mark. We three philosophers had trifled with one bush perhaps; but our share in the depredation was comparatively slight. A bell was rung, and the message read aloud. I am convinced from that moment onwards no one touched any fruit:—still the mischief had been done; it was obvious to the naked eye that the gooseberry-bushes had been attacked.

The person who seemed most distressed was poor Mlle. Zélie: she blamed no one, but repeated constantly, 'Why then did not

Madame warn me? Never should I have permitted it, had I not supposed that it was understood that these gooseberries, without value for that matter, were intended to be eaten. It seemed to me, in the absence of instructions, so natural.'

And a chorus of girls answered: 'We thought it too, Mademoiselle: never would we have touched a gooseberry had we understood.'

There the matter remained. We were not particularly unhappy: as a matter of fact all the gooseberries in the garden could have been purchased for five francs in Bruxelles. No harm had been done the bushes: it was a *mal entendu*—what would you have? The only person who seemed to take it to heart was poor Mlle. Zélie.

'Quel malheur,' she kept repeating. 'Quel malheur! mais aussi, pourquoi Madame ne m'a-t-elle rien dit?'

We continued, Marie Hazard and myself, sitting under our shady tree; our third philosopher, the Nature-worshipper, always good at decoration, had been called off to assist at laying out the tables, and arranging flowers; groups of other girls were sitting in circles on the grass or walking about arm in arm, when—suddenly arrived upon the scene M. Heger. He came up with an amiable expression: but in a moment the look changed to one black as night: he had seen the tell-tale signs of the depredations inflicted on the gooseberry-bushes.

'Who is responsible for this?' he asked, '*c'est une bassesse!* Mlle. Zélie, what does this signify? Were you not told the fruit was to be respected?'

Poor Mlle. Zélie stood there quivering with terror.

'Unhappily,' she said, 'Madame's letter arrived too late: without bad intention, these young girls imagined themselves free to eat gooseberries: from the moment it was known that it was forbidden, I am sure there was no infraction of the rule: but alas! what was done, was done. I regret it profoundly: and so I am sure do you, is it not so, my children?' she asked, turning to Marie Hazard and myself:—there was a clear and empty space around us—every other girl had somehow vanished.

'Yes, Mademoiselle, we are very sorry,' both of us answered at once.

M. Heger swooped round upon us in his wrath.

'And so,' he said, 'it is *you*, is it; you two who have so much pride, both of you; who are so little sensitive to the counsels of your teachers, you, who are so superior in your own esteem, who are the guilty ones? It is you two, and you alone in the entire Pension, who have been capable of this indignity? And see what ruin you have made! Are you not ashamed—what gluttony!'

'Mais non, Monsieur, non,' pleaded Mademoiselle Zélie, 'these young girls are not alone responsible; many others also took the fruit; you must not blame them for everything.'

'Is that so, Mademoiselle Hazard? Is that so, Mees?'

'Il ne faut pas nous demander cela,' said I, with my usual bad accent in agitated moments. 'C'est aux autres qu'il faut le demander.'

'Mais oui,' he said, 'and this is what I intend to do; Mlle. Zélie, do me this pleasure: fetch me the *élèves* who were here just now: call them together. I must get to the bottom of this. Je dois approfondir cela.'

Mlle. Zélie was some time about it: but in the end, she returned with a good company of girls, forty or fifty at least; amongst them nearly all of those who had been most busy amongst the gooseberry bushes. They stood round us in a sort of circle; Marie Hazard, myself, and M. Heger.

M. Heger delivered a little speech: he explained, and enlarged upon, the confidence that our kind hostess had placed in us; she had thrown open her garden to us; she had prepared a feast for us; she had made only one condition—respect my gooseberry-bushes. Was it possible, could one suppose it possible, that any one could be found base enough, greedy enough, to ignore her wishes?

'We were not told,' said Marie Hazard; 'This is not reasonable—one would not have touched a gooseberry had one known. Is one a child of six then, to love gooseberries to this extent?'

'Mlle. Hazard, it is not to *you* I address myself,' said M. Heger. 'I have no question to ask you. You admit, and indeed it is not possible for you to deny, that you have committed this act of gluttony—inexcusable in a child of six. It is to you all, my dear pupils, outside of these two, who I know are guilty, that I ask it, and with confidence—amongst you all, have any of you been guilty of this indignity?'

Dead silence. Mlle. Zélie was fidgeting about, snapping her fingers nervously. But she said nothing.

M. Heger again addressed the girls round him, and there was a note of triumph in his voice:—

'Cela suffit,' he affirmed, 'I shall ask no more. If any of you are guilty, you know it in your consciences: you know now what it remains for you to do. For me, I believe, and I love to believe, that the only pupil in this school capable of this unworthy conduct is a foreigner.'

'Pardon, Monsieur,' said a voice at my elbow, 'je suis Belge; et moi aussi j'ai mangé des groseilles.'

M. Heger bowed towards her profoundly.

Je fais une exception en votre faveur, Mademoiselle Hazard,' he said: and then he walked away.

I remained at first almost stupefied: the first shock rendered me unable to distinguish between reality and fiction. I began to doubt my senses: was I really, were Marie Hazard and myself, the only girls in the school who had rifled the gooseberry-bushes? Did it mean that, if not deliberately base, in some way there was a peculiar deficiency in delicacy and honour in my constitution, rendering me capable of doing base things without knowing it? Was it true that in this foreign country I had disgraced my own? This was my first impression, confusion of mind; because up to this date I had never known nor suffered from real injustice. Here was an entirely new experience. And at first it baffled me. I suppose I must have shown this desperation in my face: for M. Heger was no sooner out of sight than attempts were made to console me: but I was beyond consolation. Mlle. Zélie came first; she laid a soothing hand on my shoulder.

'Do not afflict yourself, my child,' she said. 'This is a misunderstanding: I shall explain everything to Madame Heger.'

Then several girls came bustling up, rather shamefacedly, assuring me that it was nothing: '*Quelle affaire*,' they ejaculated. '*Et tout cela à propos de quelques groseilles!*'

'It has nothing to do with the gooseberries,' I said; 'you are all cowards, and I detest you; why couldn't you say you took them too?'

'What good would it have been, with M. Heger? We shall all go to Madame and tell her everything. She will see how it is at once. *Voyons, Chou: ne pleures pas.*'

'*Je ne pleure pas; vous mentez:*' and this was both impolite and incorrect: I *was* crying, but not ordinary tears, because they scalded one.

What happens invariably with people who insist upon their own private grievances too much, and too long, happened in my case that afternoon: at first I had been an object of sympathy, but when I refused it, and was ungracious, I became a bore. The case was stated to me in reasonable terms:

'Say that we should have done differently and were cowardly. It was not out of ill-will to you, but because we were afraid of M. Heger, with whom one must not reason when he is in a bad humour, as every one knows. You and Marie Hazard, for instance, who must always be in the right with him, in what way does it serve you? Voyons: be frank; at least: *cela vous réussit-il?* Listen then: we will make it all plain with Madame Heger. Mlle. Zélie will tell her we knew nothing when we ate those gooseberries; we thought they were there for us—that it belonged to the feast to eat this fruit: they were not so very good, these gooseberries after all: it was a politeness on our part, not greediness. Every one nearly ate gooseberries. When we were told it was a mistake, we ate no more gooseberries, and were sorry. La petite Anglaise and Marie Hazard did as the others did: and here is the whole history. Now all this is known already to almost every one. It will be known to Madame Heger before we go home to-night. What then do you want? Look at Marie Hazard: she is in the same case as you are, and does not afflict herself.'

'Marie Hazard is at home here, and I am not at home. I am English; and I am told by M. Heger before you all, that because I am English I am capable of baseness.'

'And what does that do to you?' asked Marie Hazard, herself, turning upon me with her cruel reasonableness. 'English or Belgian, one is not capable of baseness, and one has not deserved any blame: that is what is serious; the rest signifies nothing. One must not be a patriot to this extent. It is not reasonable. If even you had been in the wrong about those gooseberries, do you truly imagine to yourself that the honour of England would have been affected by it?'

Just *because* this was so reasonable and true, it stung me to the soul. '*Ma chère et bonne amie*,' wrote Rousseau to Madame d'Epinay in the days of their friendship, when explaining why he had burnt a letter to her that seemed to him more reasonable than kind: '*Pythagore disait qu'il ne faut jamais attiser le feu avec une épée. Cette sentence me paraît être la plus importante et la plus sacrée des lois de l'amitié*.' I knew nothing about the sayings of Pythagoras, nor the writings of Rousseau in those days. But it did seem to me opposed to the sacred laws of friendship, to remind me, in this moment, that it was absurd in me to drag patriotism into this question.

'Leave me alone,' I said, turning my back upon them, 'you tire me, all of you; none of you understand me.'

Although I sulked the whole afternoon, and was, as I deserved to be, left to sulk, as 'insupportable,' I yet came round to the conviction before we returned, that everything had been explained, and that even M. Heger understood that an injustice had been done me; and that although, of course, no apology could be looked for from such an obstinate man, still *he knew he had been in the wrong* and was secretly repentant. But I was to be undeceived. After our return to the Rue d'Isabelle, the lecture du soir in the refectory was given, as was the usual plan on holidays, by M. Heger, seated at the head of the room, with Madame Heger on his right hand, and a table before them, placed between the two long lines of tables with benches stretching the length of the room against the walls, and two ranges of chairs on the opposite side of the tables facing the benches, where sat all the pupils. Having finished the 'reading,' M. Heger summed up in a few words the sentiments that 'he was sure all there must feel of gratitude to their hostess, once an inmate of this school; and who had contrived this little fête for her successors. He asked their consent to a message of thanks that was to be sent her; and he wound up his expression of confidence in the enjoyment every one had derived from this holiday, by stating the satisfaction of Madame Heger and himself at the good conduct of every one; and then came this sentence:—There was only one regrettable exception to be made to the perfect behaviour and sense of respect due to the lady who had thrown open her house and garden to them, and this exception, he was, at any rate, pleased to recognise, was not amongst those brought up in the sentiments of religion and convenience cherished by almost all of them: and hence though one had to deplore the fault, in the case of a foreigner (*une étrangère*) one was more disposed to regard it with indulgence.'

Marie Hazard rose from her seat:—but there really was no time for any protest or objection. There was a shuffling of chairs, a movement of benches. Monsieur and Madame Heger walked out of the Refectory by a folding door behind them that opened into a passage leading to their own part of the house; and the pupils filed out, under the surveillance of the mistress in charge, by the opposite door towards the staircase leading to the Oratory, for evening prayers. I alone remained sitting on my bench, in my usual place in the Refectory, about half-way down the right-hand line of tables. No one paid any attention to me, until the room was nearly empty, and then the mistress at the door looked round, and seeing me sitting there, said, 'Make haste, Mees; you will be late for prayers: what *are* you doing?'

I remained sitting there. She looked at me a moment; evidently didn't like my looks; shrugged her shoulders, agitated her hands, said—

'One cannot wait for you any longer mademoiselle, *vous êtes notée*,' and vanished.

I do not know now, and I hardly think I knew then, what I meant by the resolution that was the only one firmly present to me, that no one, nothing, should move me from the place where I was sitting in the Refectory: that there I was going to remain all night, and for ever if necessary, until this wrong was redressed, and until just excuses were made to me. What had at first been a new and astonishing discovery to me, that injustice could be done, and that people whom I respected and even loved, could be unjust to me, had now become a well-established and common fact, and I saw injustice everywhere and felt no use in living at all, because I had become convinced that people would always be unjust to me, *always*; it was the common rule of the world evidently. What was I to do then? Resist, perish in resisting? Very possibly, but not submit.

There I sat at fifteen years of age, on the bench, with my elbows planted on the Refectory table, and my burning, throbbing head between my hands, *in the frame of mind in which Anarchists are made.*

But the influence was already approaching that was to transform anarchy into the ideal socialism of Jean-Jacques Rousseau, where the bitter bitter rage of rebelliousness against the wrong done oneself becomes the generous sympathy with all injustice throughout the world: '*Ce premier sentiment de l'injustice est resté si profondément gravé dans mon âme, que toutes les idées qui s'y rapportent me rendent ma première émotion; et ce sentiment, relatif à moi dans son origine, a pris une telle consistance en lui-même, et s'est si bien détaché de tout intérêt personnel, que mon coeur s'enflamme au spectacle ou au récit de toute action injuste, quel qu'en soit l'objet, et en quelque lieu qu'elle se commette, comme si l'effet en retomboit sur moi.'*

The lesson that the author of the *Confessions* learnt at an even earlier age than I did was taught me by a Victim of injustice who continued throughout her life so courageously undisturbed by it in kindness and consideration for others, that her sensibility to it became a less powerful feeling in her than her compassion for the suffering and passionate woman who had wronged her.

I cannot say how long I had sat in the Refectory, when I saw the folding doors at the head of the room open, and quietly and composedly as usual, Madame Heger entered and approached me. She sat down on the chair opposite my bench on the opposite side of the table.

'My child,' she said, 'you are wrong to take so seriously the reproach addressed to you by M. Heger as the result of a mistake. Mlle. Zélie has explained to M. Heger and to me the accident. It was a pity, no doubt, that this happened: but you have not any more blame than the others. All is forgotten and forgiven. But you, my child, are wrong in this. Why do you remain here, when prayers are already over, and without permission? You know well it is forbidden.'

I broke out passionately complaining that I could not be expected to obey rules when I was unjustly treated: I could bear anything else, but I could not support injustice.

'Pas l'injustice,' I protested, 'j'obéirais a tout, je supporterais tout: mais, pas l'injustice, non, madame, non, je ne saurais supporter l'injustice.'

'Cependant, mon enfant, il faut savoir la supporter. Que faire? *Seriez-vous la seule personne au monde qui ne connaîtrait pas l'injustice?'*

I shook my head obstinately: I made a show of resistance: but I was already under Madame Heger's influence. A tremendous change had taken place in me. I was no longer an Anarchist. It had already come to me as a conviction that there was nothing grand, but rather something mean, in refusing to bear anything that my other fellow-creatures had to bear, that better and nobler people than I had borne.

'It saddens me,' continued Madame Heger—'(*Cela m'attriste*) to see a young girl like you, who soon must enter life, and who takes the habit of saying, "I cannot support this, everything else you like, *but not this*": or "I will renounce everything else, *but not that*." It does not depend upon us, my child, what we must support, nor what we may, because *les convenances* or the interests of others demand it, have to renounce. Amongst the many pupils I have known, there have been some passionate like yourself and exalted, who have said like you to-day, I cannot support injustice, who have seen injustice, where there was no intention to be unjust; who have refused counsel with anger and impatience, and who in their refusal to bow to necessary obligations have been themselves unjust. And they have been unhappy in their lives; most unhappy. *Dominated by some fixed idea, the slave of some desire that cannot be accomplished,*they have seen enemies in those who would have been their friends. They have created for themselves a sad fate; and I know one of them who died of it (*j'en connais une qui en est morte*).'

Something in Madame Heger's voice surprised me, for her even tones quavered and broke. I looked up suddenly, her face was ashen white and her lips blue. I was struck to the heart. I knew not why, but in some way I instinctively felt that, through my fault, she was in pain: I was full of remorse. The table was between us, or I should have thrown myself upon my knees before her. My emotion had the usual effect upon my French accent. 'Forgive me, oh forgive me,' I wanted to say, 'I am ashamed of myself.' I said, 'Pardong, O pardong, j'ai honte de moi.'

As it happened, nothing could have been better timed than my relapse into English barbarism. In a moment Madame's unusual emotion was under control: the soft colour returned to her cheek and lips, she shook her head gently, and said in her ordinary voice—

'You *must* take care of your accent, my child. One says

"pardon," not "pardong "; and one does not say "J'ai honte de moi," but one says "Je suis honteuse," or "J'ai honte."

'But I see you are now in a good disposition,' she went on, 'and I am pleased to see it. Thus then, go quietly to bed without disturbing your companions, and I will send Clothilde to you with some flower-of-orange water that will tranquillise this hot head. Good night, and be very wise in the future: and all will be well.'

Ever since I have known the story of Charlotte Brontë I have had the firm conviction of what was in Madame Heger's mind when she spoke to me of one who had imagined enemies in friends, and who, complaining of injustice, had been unjust. But since I have read Charlotte's Letters, the unmistakable proof is that Madame Heger, so far as my memory serves me after all these years, actually quoted the very words of one of these letters, about one dominated by a fixed idea, and the slave of vain desires.

So then we may decide finally, that Madame Heger was not Madame Beck. And of M. Heger we may decide that he was not Paul Emanuel either; for Paul Emanuel having learnt that he had committed an injustice, would have called his whole school together, and in full class-room repaired his involuntary fault. But the real M. Heger did nothing of the sort. For a time there was a great coldness towards him in my heart. But in the hours of his lessons he remained, as ever, the 'Professor' of unrivalled merit.

Summing up what may be gathered from these reminiscences, I think the facts that can be affirmed are these:—

No moral likeness, but a physical resemblance, between Madame Heger and the portrait of Madame Beck. A strong and lifelike resemblance, between Paul Emanuel and M. Heger, up to the point when the Professor Paul falls in love with Lucy Snowe. After this event, a dwindling resemblance between the Professor in *Villette*, and the real Professor in the Rue d'Isabelle, who was never in love with Charlotte Brontë, and who was the lawful and attached husband of the Directress of the Pensionnat.

But when Professor Paul Emanuel becomes the docile disciple of Père Silas, when he is caught in the 'Jesuitical cobwebs of mother Church,' then he ceases to resemble the real man in the very least. M. Heger's role in life was not that of a disciple but of a Master of other people, and a very arbitrary and domineering Master too, for whom the world was his class-room. He was under the thumb of no priest, nor spiritual director. As for Jesuitical 'cobwebs,' the notion of M. Heger caught in any cobweb is absurd!

Every one knows what happens when a bumble-bee in its courses comes in contact with a cobweb. It is a mere incident in the career of the bumble-bee—but it is a disaster for the cobweb.

www.ingramcontent.com/pod-product-compliance
Lightning Source LLC
Chambersburg PA
CBHW032228080426
42735CB00008B/765
9781528703987